All-Terrain Bikes

by the editors of *Bicycling*® Magazine

Rodale Press, Emmaus, Pennsylvania

Printed in the United States of America on recycled paper, con-
taining a high percentage of de-inked fiber.

Senior Editor, Ray Wolf
Edited by Larry McClung
Cover photograph by Mark Lenny
Cover design by Linda Jacopetti and Karen A. Schell
Book design by Linda Jacopetti

Library of Congress Cataloging in Publication Data
Main entry under title:

All-terrain bikes.

  Cover title: Bicycling magazine's all-terain bikes.
  1. All terrain bicycles. 2. All terrain cycling.
I. Bicycling! II. Title: Bicycling magazine's all-
terrain bikes.
TL410.A424 1985 629.28'472 85-2258
ISBN 0-87857-546-4 paperback

2 4 6 8 10 9 7 5 3 1 paperback

Contents

Introduction

The first half of the decade of the 80s has been an interesting period for bicycle enthusiasts. Stiff competition in the recreational bicycle market, coupled with favorable exchange rates for products manufactured in Europe and the Far East, has led to the availability in the United States of high-quality bikes at prices affordable for most buyers. Along with this general move toward mass-production of quality bikes, there has been the development of new types of bikes—most notably the all-terrain bikes (ATB), which have generated much of the excitement in the market during the last couple of years. Though these bikes have their unique features, they have shared in the benefits of the high technology that has led to mass-production of lightweight, alloy frames and components for bikes of all types.

Much of the allure of the ATB comes from its adaptability to all sorts of environments. You can ride your ATB to and from work during the week, then use it on the weekend to retreat to the beauty and serenity of wild and natural places. You can ride it down city streets, along the beach, or up into the mountains. This type of bike is not only highly practical, it is loads of fun as well.

The all-terrain bike originated in the Western part of the United States, in an area north of San Francisco blessed with an abundance of mountains criss-crossed by fire roads and hiking trails. The ATB evolved in response to the desire of bike lovers to develop two-wheelers that can be navigated over such rugged terrain, which is lethal to skinny-tired racing and touring bikes.

One of the great attractions of most back roads and mountain trails is that they are little used, hence relatively free from traffic. They provide the cyclist with relief from the constant necessity to be on the lookout for other, potentially dangerous, vehicles. In the back country, one can travel for miles in quiet reflection and communion with the natural world, listening to sounds of birds, observing the land, enjoying scenic vistas. Riding in such areas is the cycling equivalent of backpacking.

The rugged construction, multiple gearing, and comfortable ride of the all-terrain bike also make it a choice touring vehicle. This is especially true when a tour is planned for areas where one is likely to encounter a wide variety of road surfaces. As we will see later in this book, an increasing number of touring organizations are offering tours specifically intended for ATB use, along with their regular selection of tours. And several new businesses have begun that specialize in off-road tours, among them some who offer tours in places like China and Nepal.

Racing and touring bikes will always have their place, of course, but they are meant for pavement—their thrill is speed. ATBs offer a different set of thrills—versatility, access to new worlds and new environments, the chance to ride slowly over rocks and logs in quiet places as well as briskly down a city street. They offer freedom, the chance to rough it, to be a kid again.

The Editors,
Bicycling magazine

Part One
The Development of the All-Terrain Bike

The Race That Gave Birth to the Clunker

It is a cool, clear morning in Northern California. Five young men sweat as they push strangely modified bicycles up a steep hill. They are discussing the dirt road surface, which resembles a moonscape more than it does a road. These men belong to the same breed that ski down cliffs, jump out of airplanes, or ride skateboards down Everest; they have developed their own unique athletic challenge, a race known only to a few dozen locals and referred to as "Repack." The road they are on is the racecourse.

At the top of the hill, where the road intersects another rarely used fire road, the 5 men are met by another 15 riders, including a couple of high-energy women. Most of the crowd are in their twenties, but there are a few teenagers and one bearded individual who claims to be 50. No one believes him. All are wearing heavy shirts and pants, and most have leather gloves and Vibram-soled boots.

There seems to be a little method to this madness, however, as one of the group drags a well-thumbed notebook out of a backpack along with a pair of electronic stopwatches. The notebook is the heart of the race, since it contains all previous race results as well as the phone numbers of the local riders. (Races are not scheduled; they are held only when the cosmic alignment is right.)

Names are taken, and numbers are assigned according to experience, and each rider is then assigned a starting time. The list is copied, and the watches are started simultaneously. A scruffy looking official timer takes a watch and a copy of the list, jumps on his machine, and vanishes downhill.

Riders eat oranges, make minor adjustments, and talk excitedly among themselves. Finally, the first name is called, and a nervous young man wheels up to the starting line scraped in the dirt. This is his first time down the course. He spends his last few seconds at the top asking questions about the course and not listening to the answers.

"Ten seconds ... five seconds." The novice is so anxious that he applies full power a little early; however, the starter has a firm grasp on the rear wheel and releases it as he says "Go!" The novice is thrown off balance by his early start and wobbles for the first few yards before finding the throttle and disappearing over the first rise.

The Birth of a New Sport?

These racers have no idea whether their sport will catch on with the public at large, but they are enjoying it too much to give that much thought. Their bicycles are as unique as their sport; mostly old Schwinns, with a few other rugged species included. All are highly modified. Most are 5- or 10-speeds with front and rear drum brakes, motorcycle brake levers, motocross bars, and the biggest knobby tires available.

A few reactionaries still cling to their 1- or 2-speed coaster brake machines, but drum brakes and 10-speeds seem to be the wave of the future among these off-road racers. The machines are called Clunkers, Bombers, or Cruisers, depending on the owner's local affiliation, and on this day in the late 1970s, there are no more than a few hundred of the advanced models in Northern California—far fewer still in the rest of the world.

Clunking in Marin County

Clunking (riding a bike over rough, unpaved terrain) probably started with the invention of the bicycle, since people have been riding old bikes on dirt roads ever since there were old bikes and dirt roads to ride on. The significance of Marin County

Photograph 1–1. An early model, custom-built clunker from Marin County, complete with laterals and fork-reinforcement bars and weighing a hefty 45 pounds.

for the history of clunking is that there, in the mid to late 1970s, something new and distinctive emerged. Old bikes were successfully crossed with 10-speed bikes to produce a hybrid product perfectly adapted to the fire roads and trails of the Northern California hills. In the process of field testing modifications, the researchers shattered every part to be found on a bicycle. Rims, hubs, handlebars, cranks, seatposts, saddles, gears, chains, derailleurs, stems, pedals, and frames—all were ground to fragments along with the exterior portions of a number of clunking enthusiasts.

Early in the experimental stage, the hill now known as Repack was recognized as the ultimate field test for bike and rider. To get to this hill, racers loaded their balloon-tired Schwinn clunkers into the back of a pickup truck and drove up the north slope of Marin County's Mount Tamalpais until the truck could go no farther. From there they pedaled up to the top of what was then called the Cascades fire road and is now officially called Repack Road.

Repack Road drops 1,300 feet in 1.8 miles, averaging about

a 14 percent grade. Various sections present dirt, gravel, football-size boulders, 20 percent slopes, and rutted gnarly stretches of bare rock. It serves as the course for an exciting, if brief, downhill race. In the early days, everyone used coaster brakes. By the time a rider made it to the bottom of the hill, all the grease in his coaster brake had turned to smoke. The brake was sizzling hot and had to be repacked with grease. That's how the hill got its name.

The early crazies weren't completely mad, so after some preliminary runs, they decided that the course was better suited for individual time trials than for a massed-start race. An official would pedal down the course, stopwatch in pocket, and time the riders as they crossed the finish line. Racers were sent off at two-minute intervals to prevent one rider from catching another, since passing on this course is not easy. Racers were grouped by ability to prevent a slow rider from being followed by a fast rider who might catch up. The fastest riders started last so the others could see the experts finish.

The race was run fairly regularly through 1979. By then a good Sunday would see as many as 50 bikes, including a few custom-made prototype ATBs. Fifteen-speed gear trains were added so riders could pedal back for a second run. In 1979, Gary Fisher set the record time of 4 minutes, 22 seconds, and Joe Breeze was one second slower.

With the 1979 rainy season, the Repack races ceased. Part of the reason was the increased policing from the Marin Municipal Water District rangers. Outlaw ATBers were making nuisances of themselves on the hiking and horse trails. But, the main reason was that many of the original organizers had become ATB entrepreneurs. Gary Fisher, Charlie Kelly, Joe Breeze, and Eric Koski were spending their weekends designing, building, and selling the prototype MountainBikes, Breezers, and Trailmasters.

Repack Revisited

Frank Berto, *Bicycling* magazine's gear expert and contributing editor, is a Bay area resident. He admits that he watched the development of custom-built clunkers with complete disbe-

Photograph 1–2. Repack Road—race course and test laboratory for the development of the all-terrain bicycle.

lief. He thought the off-road bikes of Marin County would go the way of hula hoops and pet rocks. He didn't believe the movement started by the kamikaze racers on Repack Road would survive, until he noticed that every tenth bike in Marin County was an ATB.

Late in the summer of 1983, Berto saw a flier in a bike shop that announced: "Repack is Back. Competition will be staged on October 8 for a new Repack record; sanctioned by NORBA (National Off-Road Bicycle Association)." Seized by a return of youthful curiosity, he decided to enter the race, reasoning that someone had to come in last.

Frank borrowed a Ritchey MountainBike from Gary Fisher the day before the race. It was an early model, but the gear train was very much to Berto's tastes. It had 28/38/48 Shimano Biopace chainwheels on 180-mm Sugino Aero Tour cranks. This was combined with a 14–16–18–21–28–38 SunTour New Winner freewheel, a DID chain, and SunTour derailleurs. He switched the brakes from right-hand front to the conventional pattern. Everything else was stock.

From this point on we will let Frank Berto describe his experiences as a late-blooming gonzo racer in his own words.

The Rover Boys on Repack

On Saturday morning, I put on my racing uniform: Bell Tourlite helmet, Levi pants and jacket, high boots, and a pair of leather gloves. I had never pedaled Repack, so I decided to inspect the course before the race. I pedaled the five miles from my home to the finish line in Fairfax and alternately pedaled and walked up Repack. The bike was geared low enough to climb the 20 percent slopes, but I couldn't convert oatmeal to glycogen fast enough to pedal all the way.

I found that it takes a nice bit of balance to climb steep dirt trails. Lean too far forward and the rear wheel spins; too far back, and the front wheel does a wheelie. I had to climb sitting in the saddle. If I stood up, the front and rear wheels would alternately lose traction. It took me 45 minutes to make it to the top.

The starting line was a typical "mellow Marin" mob scene. There were TV crews from two stations and numerous people with expensive cameras and notebooks. There were also a formidable 60 entrants, with team members from Ross, Specialized Bicycle Imports, and the S. E. motocross racing team from Los Angeles. Many of the early Repack riders, including Joe Breeze, Otis Guy, Gary Fisher, and Bob Burrows, were there to defend their records. Finally, there were these strange bearded characters in jeans, T-shirts, beer bellies, and coaster brake Goodwill specials. On a one to ten scale, I was ten for equipment, five for appearance, and one for experience.

The race started an hour late. Charlie Kelly, the starter, gave the race invocation: "If you crash and break a few bones, wait for the first aid crew. Unless you're blocking the good line; if so, then try to drag yourself off to one side. If you see somebody down on the course and bleeding, stop and give help—unless you're on a real good run. Then, shout at the next first aid man."

The timer ticked down to zero, and the first racer blasted off. I took my camera and walked down to the first "wipe-out" corner. The next rider, Glen Brown (Zzipper Fairings), approached at terminal velocity and slid off the road end over end. He got up, inspected himself and his bike for loose pieces, and carried on. I noted that first aiders and radio hams were stationed about every quarter mile.

The radio at the starting line was alternately reporting crashes and top times. The TV crews headed down the course to where the turkey vultures were circling. The waiting racers were going through a tire-pinching exercise. The object is to have soft tires for best traction, but not too soft. Pinch-pssst. Pinch-pssst. A few riders wore shorts, cycling shoes, toe clips, and straps. Think positive.

As the minutes and the riders ticked away, I thought, "Berto, aren't you a bit too old for this? But, you've already had your TV interview, so you can't gracefully chicken out."

Five minutes to go. Lower the saddle. Cinch up the helmet. On with the gloves. Set up in middle gear.

"Number 56."

I push up to the starting line.

"Fifteen seconds."

"Five seconds."

"Go!"

Musings during a Tour Down Repack Road

Push off.

Pedal like crazy down the first 200 yards of level road. Over the edge. First turn approaching. Let's not wipe out on the first corner like Glen Brown.

Get over the rear wheel. Brake! Boy, the front brake really stops, but the rear just skids the back wheel.

Hold your line. Don't hit that gully. Too late! Wham! Crunch! Gosh, nothing broke. Amazing. If this were a skinny-tire bike, it would be in three pieces.

Gulp! I'll never make this turn. Brake hard! Hold the rear brake on! Slide! What a pounding.

I know the last part is worst. It has those steep tight corners that slope the wrong way. Here comes the worst curve.

Look at that mob of spectators—and they all have cameras. I'm going way too fast. If I'm going to wipe out, let's go down in style.

Lock the rear brake. Right foot down. Slide!

"Go for it, Frank!" shouts a friend. Bump! Bump! Thump! Hang on!

Photograph 1–3. One of the great challenges of the downhill Repack race course is negotiating the many tight turns without wiping out.

Unreal. I didn't fall. I haven't slid like that since I was 15. Pedal! Pedal! There's the finish line!

Finish Line

The timer says "Number 56: 6 minutes, 18 seconds." There are several hundred people at the finish. Slowly, my adrenaline winds down.

The last two riders are the course record holders: Joe Breeze and Gary Fisher. Joe crosses the line in 4 minutes, 44 seconds. Everyone waits for Gary. He crosses the line in 5 minutes, 29 seconds with grease on his white gloves. The chain came off when he skidded into a bush.

The winning times are announced. Two young riders from Roseville, Jim Denton (4:41) and Mike Jordan (4:45), come in first and third. A and B Cycle, their sponsor will be celebrating. Joe Breeze is second. Ten riders are under 5 minutes. Marcus

Gannister of the SBI team is the top novice at 4:58. Denise
Carmagna, the editor of *Fat Tyre Flyer,* is the top woman at 7:10.

So, the old Repack record still stands. Maybe it's waiting
for you. Or, perhaps the new Over 50—Novice record of 6:18
is more your style. I'll see you there.

The Vanguard: ATBs and Their California Builders

Although the concept has now spread worldwide, northern
California and specifically Marin County, just north of San Francisco, have taken credit for starting the "fat tire" or "all-terrain"
bicycle movement. True, people in other areas have indepen-
dently arrived at similar ideas, and as early as 1953, John Finley
Scott built an off-road bicycle on a Schwinn diamond frame that
looked remarkably similar to bikes on the market today, but the
idea failed to take off at that time.

Perhaps a movement of this type needed a certain California
craziness to get off the ground. At any rate, northern Californian
influence can be traced through all its stages to the current state
of the art, and the process is still going on via a cadre of dedicated
and imaginative bike builders.

During the late 1960s and early 1970s, a number of forces
in the American culture and economy had helped to create a
bike boom. By the mid 1970s, bicycles were quite popular, but
they were still a long way from practical; the more one spent
on a bike, the less substantial it seemed to be.

In this context, the development of the all-terrain bike may
have been unavoidable, since it arose to meet the practical needs
of a group of bicycle enthusiasts. The all-terrain design evolved
spontaneously through a series of unplanned steps in which
parts on conventional bikes were broken and replaced with
stronger or newly fabricated ones. Eventually, a bike with its

own special identity emerged. No longer a makeshift vehicle, it was just as sophisticated as those built for travel on paved roads.

Recently, Charlie Kelly, a West Coast contributing editor for *Bicycling* magazine who is himself an important figure in the ATB movement, spoke to four prominent California builders about their influences and ideas and discovered an interesting diversity within the group. The development of the ATB has caused so much change in the bicycle industry and in the way people look at bicycles that Charlie finds it difficult to say exactly how much credit these men deserve for bringing about this change. Perhaps they simply responded to needs that were bound to be filled by someone. But at the very least, the ATB can be described as the result of a fortunate match of resourceful people and appropriate times.

Roadies and Gonzos

The two major cycling influences present in Marin County in the early 1970s were the traditional roadie types and the more outlaw, 1-speed, downhill coasters. Although each group regarded the other with something akin to suspicion, interaction between the two was inevitable. From the gonzos came the tradition of off-road insanity, and from the roadies came the equipment innovations and the desire to ride up as well as down hills.

As a result, the two groups merged slightly, and by 1976 the Marin County "clunker" was a unique breed of bike found nowhere else in such numbers. With an old Schwinn frame (preferably from the Excelsior series), drum brakes, huge motorcycle handlebars, motorcycle brake levers, chrome "fork braces," thumb shifters or perhaps a pair of stem shifters next to one grip, Brooks B-72 saddle, one-piece cranks (or the occasional TA), the whole package weighed 50 pounds.

But as the sport of clunking grew, the supply of good, old frames was shrinking as more and more fell apart from off-road abuse, and the cost of replacing one almost justified a custom frame. At this point, a new breed of bike tinkerers and frame builders began to set their own course in the development of yet another all-American product.

Photograph 1–4. Joe Breeze, creator of the first custom bike for rough terrain, at work in his shop.

Joe Breeze

Joe Breeze deserves credit for producing the first successful custom fat-tire bicycle made for rough country, and all of the ten frames he built in 1977 are still in use. Joe had taken Albert Eisentraut's frame building course, had built several road frames, and possessed other good qualifications. He had registered some of the fastest times on the Repack downhill race course, thus he knew something about handling, and he was and is an exacting craftsman—too exacting almost. It took eight months from the first exchange of money until his first custom bikes were completed, but in that time Breeze literally reinvented the wheel.

Among his innovations were the first use of oversize tubing for ATBs (using a 1⅛-inch down tube for a top tube), the use of motorcycle handlebars, and the use of a bottom bracket made for a standard balloon-tire bicycle on an ATB.

Here's how Breeze tells his story: "I was interested in restoring old bikes. Right around that same time I started building road frames, and I wanted to get some of these old bikes and restore something like that Columbia shaft-drive. So while we went to different road races around the state, we would always check out old barns, old bike shops, and try to track down these old bikes. Down in Santa Cruz at this old shop we went through this deep, deep pile going back in time. We finally got down to the late thirties and early forties and picked out this Schwinn; it was actually the Excelsior design—what we call a short Excelsior. It was spray painted red and had fenders and a big wire basket; the guy wanted five dollars for it, so I went for it.

"Some of my friends had been riding on the mountain on old fat-tire bikes, and I had friends from back in high school who had these Speedo bikes that they got from the dumps for basic transportation. I used to look at those and say, 'Inefficient, forget it; you know skinny tires and drop handlebars are the way to go.' One of my friends had this old bike, a '47 Schwinn, but the tires were pumped up and the chain was oiled, so I just hopped on it to see what this was all about, and I said, 'Wow, this is great!' Nice stable feel, like the difference between ballet (on the skinny-tire bike) and football (on the fat-tire bike).

"So I went home and I scraped the red paint off my Schwinn Excelsior, and it had the original beautiful two-tone paint job with the feather heads around the head tube. I was just going to restore it, but a couple of my friends talked me into hitch-hiking to the top of the mountain with it. We rode down this old railroad grade, and it was incredible, so I really got into it.

"These Excelsior designs seemed to handle pretty well. It had the best geometry for this type of riding, and we spent a lot of time hitchhiking up the mountain with our bikes to ride down. Then after a while, because we were in pretty good shape from road racing, we started riding farther and farther up the mountain before hitchhiking until eventually we would just ride to the top. The gearing was 52/20, and that's a pretty tall gear to be riding uphill; even though we were in good shape, it got old.

"A bunch of guys from my bike club got into the old bikes, and eventually gears were put on them. Gary (Fisher) had a lot to do with that, as well as being the person who put the quick-release on the seatpost. So the gears came into play, and there were people riding around on these old bikes with gears.

"Some of my friends approached me to build some frames, so I said, 'Yeah, I'll build ten and see how it goes,' and before they were half done, they were all sold. They were pretty much the Excelsior design because I wanted to start with something that I knew worked for what we were doing, which was all-around transportation-type bike riding. I associated the curved tubes with straight ones, and instead of using mild steel tubing I used chrome-moly, bigger diameter tubes with thinner walls. The first ten had twin laterals, but later on I incorporated some of that weight into a bigger diameter down tube and thicker chainstays for a bike that was ¾ to 1 pound lighter but was just as strong and stiff and had ten fewer welds.

"Those bikes had a 68-degree head angle and 70-degree seat, around a 44-inch wheelbase with 18½-inch chainstays and a 2-inch fork offset. The bikes I build now are pretty much the same, except that I've steepened the head angle, and the chain-stays are a little shorter."

In 1978, Breeze and Otis Guy wanted to set a cross-country record on a tandem, so they went to frame builder Tom Ritchey for a special bike. Breeze describes what happened when Ritchey saw his new all-terrain bike: "His eyes lit up, and he said, 'That's great!' "

Tom Ritchey

Tom Ritchey began building bikes when he was a teenage cycling wunderkind. He jokes that the first frame he built when he was fourteen was going to ". . . revolutionize bike building. I raced on that bike and actually won, but I wouldn't ride it now." Ritchey was a talented racer and attended the Junior World's Championship race in Poland when he was seventeen.

One of the more amusing anecdotes of Ritchey's racing career occurred when he was sixteen. He entered the 90-mile Crockett-Martinez road race and won it with a solo breakaway that left no doubt as to who was the strongest rider in the field. When the USCF officials found out his age, he was disqualified for being too young, and the prize was given to a rider who had arrived at the line several minutes after Ritchey. The pressures of traveling to races and the absence of any tangible rewards discouraged him from staying on the circuit as an adult. So, he has applied his talents to frame building since his late teens.

Ritchey is definitely one person who has done quite well in the field of fat tires. As a single frame builder making hand-crafted off-road bikes, he is far ahead of whoever is in second place in production, and his designs have heavily influenced the direction of the industry. Working once again from the design of the Schwinn Excelsior and adding the influence of Breeze's bikes along with his own ideas, Ritchey began making his best-known bikes in 1979.

Many of Ritchey's innovations have become common in the industry. Among them are the one-piece triangulated handlebar; the seat tube ovalized at the bottom bracket; curved, tapered fork blades; and oversize top and down tubes. Although his off-road bikes have evolved significantly in five years, Ritchey claims that he is doing little that is really new. He prefers to be regarded as a conservative frame builder.

"These are really traditional bikes, built with modern methods," he says. "I started with these bikes by copying an old Schwinn design . . . how conservative can you get? The principles of building bikes have been researched for 75 years or more, and by now there isn't much that hasn't been tried in available materials, tubing diameters, and so on. For some reason the chrome-moly steel frame, with a certain size tubing, has been the one design that has lasted, and there must be a reason.

Photograph 1–5. Tom Ritchey, out for a pleasure ride on one of his handcrafted ATBs.

"My design has evolved from the geometry I started with, though. The first bikes were 68 to 70, but now I use 68½ to 72 for my regular bikes and 69 to 73 for the racing model. The problem with the shallow seat angle is that it puts the weight too far back for the climbs."

Ritchey believes building lugless bicycles made it easier for him to experiment with his first bikes. "Because I've always worked lugless, it was easy to put together these new bikes, using unusual tubing sizes (oversize top and down tubes, stays made of straight-gauge tubing) and angles. Most frame builders use lugs, and production bikes wouldn't be possible without lugs. But for the strongest frame, brazing is the best way, especially for mountain bikes that take more abuse than road bikes."

Ritchey feels that the finish of a bike says a lot about its builder. He points out the scalloped seat cluster reinforcement on one of his bikes: "That scallop is done carefully to get the perfect French curve. That's my art, little touches like that. I've even seen other frame builders try to copy this scallop, and they don't seem to understand the lines of it; they make the point too sharp or too blunt, they don't radius it right. . . ."

As a person who has immersed himself in bicycles since his early teens, Ritchey believes that a real dedication to the subject is essential to building quality bicycles. "So many people learn to weld in an auto shop, and they decide to reinvent the wheel by building a completely new kind of bike. I don't think a lot of them understand how beautifully the forces are balanced in the designs that have been around for so long. Even though my bikes are designed in a new direction, I don't think I'm doing anything really new; I'm just trying to complement a tradition that's been around a lot longer than I have."

Steve Potts

Steve Potts has a reputation as a meticulous craftsman among off-road frame builders. That's not surprising since he and Ritchey are good friends. Potts says, "I've been messing around with torches since I was about thirteen —silver soldering and brazing and so on. When I was in high school I used to work in the metal shop, repairing old bikes and fixing them up." Potts tried his hand at motorcycle racing, playing drums, and sheet-metal work, but his life turned around in 1980 when he and Breeze toured New Zealand on a pair of Breeze's ATBs. Potts got so excited about the new bikes that he decided to try his hand at the thing he loved most. In 1981, he built his first ATB, a present for a friend, and he hasn't looked back since.

With a smaller output than Ritchey's, Potts and business partner Mark Slate take a personal interest in each of their cus-

Photograph 1–6. Steve Potts, holding one of his carefully designed and constructed frames.

tomers, and in Marin county, Potts's bikes have a strong follow-ing. Potts gives Ritchey credit for being one of his strongest influences when he started building frames. "Even though we're kind of competitors," says Potts, "I go over to Tom's house and we bounce ideas off each other. He taught me a lot of what I know about building bikes."

Working with his friend Slate, Potts has taken his bikes into his own creative areas, experimenting with geometry and han-dlebar designs as well as looking into different ways to join the tubing. One of his means of strengthening a frame is to slip a short piece of tubing into the end of the down tube where it is attached to the head tube. "We make the internal tube a really close fit, and then when we put it on the head tube it wicks the brass up inside for a really strong joint." This process is not used on every bike. "We only do it on bikes that are going to need it for big or strong riders. Then the whole bike is built with the extra strength in mind. It wouldn't be right to do it to a small bike because it would change the way the bike worked."

Potts and Slate feel that they are in the process of fine-tuning their bike designs, and both prefer to ride a little steeper head angle than on the bikes they normally sell. "It's really precise handling," Potts says. "Not 'quick,' just precise; it goes where you point it. 'Quick' implies that it could sweep you off at any moment."

"Mark's bike and my bike are a little steeper and a little shorter and probably not for everybody, but I like it just fine. Ours have 71-degree head angles, but for most people 70 degrees with the wheelbase we're using is just right. Our wheelbase is from 41½ inches up to 44 inches, depending on the size of the bike. A lot of bikes go through different sizes and have the same chainstay lengths. Every one of ours is different, and it makes a lot more work for us because the differences are small. It has to be done in a balanced manner; you can't just change one thing and leave everything else alone. Everyone is a different size and they'll sit on the bike differently, and the weight will be in a different place if you don't take that into account."

In addition to their frames, Potts and Slate have a number of components either in production or on the drawing board, including new stems, seatpost designs, and brakes. Still, they give credit to the roots of their interest. "The original design everybody used is off Joe's conception of the Schwinn Excelsior, so you know it all evolves. We're all standing on each other's shoulders, learning things from each other. We didn't design anything new, we just refined a few things. But where most bicycle companies are conservative, we try a lot of new things, although we're not off-the-wall radicals with a lot of crazy ideas."

Charlie Cunningham

Although Charlie Cunningham builds his own frames, he is loosely associated with Potts and Slate in a group effort called Wilderness Trail Bikes and is a codeveloper of some of their new components. For example, he helped develop a new braking system for ATBs, the "roller-cam" brake, which is manufactured by SunTour. Cunningham's approach to off-road bikes draws on years of cycling and his experience as an aerospace engineer.

Working as a carpenter, Cunningham commuted over Marin County fire roads on a "skinny-tire" bike until the fat-tire revolution that was going on around him became too attractive to resist. Cunningham builds only a few dozen frames a year, not many compared to the standards of some builders. He chooses to build a limited number of frames and to take special care to make sure each rider-purchaser is happy with the product. As limited-production items, Cunningham's bicycles are among the most expensive ATBs on the market, with framesets averaging around $1,500.

Cunningham's bikes are as radical a departure as seems possible from the other off-road designs. His choice of material is oversize aluminum tubing, which is put together in configurations that most cyclists will find unconventional. Also, some of the components are of his own design or are standard components modified for his designs. Many of his off-road bicycles are equipped with drop handlebars in contrast to the flat, motorcycle-style bars more commonly used.

"Heat-treated, oversize aluminum tubes have not been used

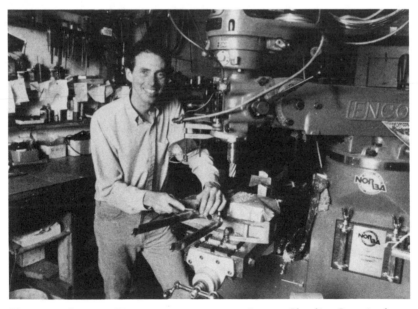

Photograph 1–7. Former aerospace engineer, Charlie Cunningham, working on one of his limited production, oversize aluminum tubed frames.

for off-road frames on a significant scale, so there is little prior design experience to draw from," he says. "This puts special importance on the necessity of excellent engineering from the outset. I feel that aluminum, if properly engineered, will in time be widely accepted as the ideal material for high performance bike frames. It's already used in almost all components.

"There is a responsibility that accompanies involvement with oversized aluminum in its early stages of development, and that is to ensure that it gains an impeccable reputation as a frame material as the years go by. I expect my customers to share with me information derived from the use of their bikes under all conditions. One way I test bikes is to build intentionally underdesigned bikes, which are tested by carefully chosen riders to find out where the trouble areas might be."

Cunningham is proud of his bikes' durability and performance. "My bikes have an excellent reputation for doing what off-road bikes are supposed to do, and they're guaranteed for the lifetime of the owner."

Currently, Cunningham is using three designs: the "Indian," a general riding frame with the relaxed angles and slightly longer wheelbase reminiscent of the Excelsior-based designs; a racing frame with stiffer forks, shorter wheelbase, and steeper angles; and a "little people's bike" for riders with short legs. As an example of how one thing leads to another, the roller-cam brake design is necessary for some of Cunningham's frames that have short seatstays. On these frames, a conventional cantilever brake would be in the way of the rider's heels, but the roller-cam does not project from the frame and is mounted under the chainstays instead of the seatstay.

Cunningham points out that in spite of some nontraditional characteristics, his "Indian" touring model is built up with standard off-the-shelf components. "While my racing bikes have custom or custom-modified components, the touring models can be worked on in any bike shop between here and Timbuktu. Everything is standard—headset, bottom bracket, derailleurs and hubs." There is, however, a long list of options for riders who want them, including custom forks, brakes, stem, handlebars, hubs, and toe clips—all products of Cunningham's desire to build the best bike he can, regardless of the limits imposed on him by component manufacturers.

Aside from the fact that they are on the cutting edge of off-road bicycle technology and chose different approaches to their off-road vehicles, the common element among these builders is their creative attitude toward bicycle building. While they may protest that they have only carried on in the tradition of other frame builders, each of these artists has put his mark on his chosen field, as have the many other builders and enthusiasts who have helped make these new bikes into the most versatile form of two-wheel transportation yet devised.

The Man Behind Mountain Bikes

This story would not be complete without some mention of Gary Fisher, another well-known name among ATB enthusiasts, because of his role in the development of the movement. Fisher is credited with being the first Marin County rider to put gears on his "clunker." Others had done similar things as early as 1953, but Fisher's innovation of gears on a fat-tire bike is the lineal ancestor of the modern mountain machine. Fisher also deserves credit for being the first to use "thumb shifters," the now-universal shifting mechanism for ATBs, and for introducing the seatpost quick-release—standard equipment for serious off-road cyclists.

In 1979, Gary asked Tom Ritchey to build him an off-road bike, and that request helped to open the ATB floodgates. Ritchey built not just 1 but 12 in the first couple of months. As his interest grew, Ritchey asked Gary to help him sell the bikes. The first attempt at marketing ATBs was Ritchey MountainBikes, a partnership including Fisher, Ritchey, and Charles Kelly. Most "serious" manufacturers were amused when they first saw these bikes at the trade shows, but subsequent events brought ATBs out of the novelty category and placed them firmly in the visionary column.

In the early days of the off-road racing movement, Fisher was unbeatable, winning nearly every race he entered. He is also the holder of the course record on the infamous Repack downhill race for five years (and still counting). Gary has passed the torch to his ace rider, local boy Joe Murray, who works in

Photograph 1—8. Gary Fisher, longtime record-holder in the race down Repack Road, has played important roles both in the development and the marketing of all-terrain bikes.

Fisher's bike shop when he is not on the race circuit. Murray was the hottest off-road racer in the United States in 1984.

In the past two years, Fisher has bought out his former partner Kelly and severed his relationship with Tom Ritchey as frame builder in order to take a new approach to marketing his ATBs. His company, now known as Fisher MountainBikes, features a T.I.G.-welded ATB built in Japan, the Montare. MountainBikes also has a limited production competition model with a handmade domestic frame. Although Fisher is reluctant to reveal the names of the frame builders putting them together, he says he has seven different builders working off a set of standard plans, and he is beginning to do some of the frame work himself as he gears up a frame producing capability in his shop.

Part Two
Buying and Equipping Your ATB

All-Terrain Bikes: A Buyer's Guide

When it comes to selecting an all-terrain bike, there are so many different models available that it is often difficult to know how to choose. Unless you are already quite knowledgeable about bikes and bike components, it is a good idea for you to get help. Reading road test articles and consulting the annual buyer's guide in *Bicycling* magazine is one way to get needed assistance. However, *Bicycling* is unable to review every bike on the market, so you may find bikes that interest you that are not reviewed in the magazine.

One solution to this problem is to get to know your local bicycle dealers, since in most cases they will be your best sources of information. There is a deluge of bikes and components on the market today, and bike dealers are the ones in the best position to know what is reliable and what to avoid.

Another good source for critical comment on bikes and components is a bike club. Check to see if there is a club in your area and get to know some of its members. Maybe you will even decide to join. Of course, everything you read and hear is a matter of opinion—informed opinion perhaps, but opinion nonetheless—so it is also important to develop and learn to exercise your own critical judgment. In order to do that, it helps to be familiar with the variety of materials used in the manufacture of bicycles and components and to have some sense of their relative merits.

Frame Materials

A bicycle's frame is usually made either from straight-gauge mild steel, straight-gauge or butted alloy steel, or (in a few cases) aluminum. What you need to know, then, is how these materials differ and why you might prefer one over another.

Mild, or high-tensile, steel is seldom used in good-quality bicycle frames, and you'll have to look hard to find it in bicycles priced above $250. Because the strength of mild steel is considerably lower than that of steel alloys, high-tensile steel frames are made of thicker, and subsequently heavier, tubes. Although such a frame may be very stiff, it won't possess any of the liveliness and shock absorption that is characteristic of an alloy steel frame.

Next up on the quality scale is alloy steel tubing. The most commonly preferred alloys are *chrome-molybdenum,* or chrome-moly (used in Columbus, Tange Champion, and Ishiwata tubing), and *manganese-molybdenum* (used in Reynolds 531 tubing). *Carbon-manganese* alloys (found in Tange Mangaloy, Ishiwata Mangy-X, Vitus 181 and 888, and Fuji Valite tubing) are less expensive and only a little less strong than the other high-strength steel alloys.

The use of any of these alloys, even in straight-gauge form and only for the three main tubes of the bicycle frame, is a significant step up in quality from a high-tensile steel frame. Extending the use of high-strength alloys to the fork blades, chainstays, and seatstays will further improve the quality of the frame.

The final quantum leap in steel frame quality involves the use of butted tubing. This type of tube has a thinner-walled center section than its straight-gauge counterparts. The butting process allows the tube walls to be made thicker at both ends, where greater strength is needed, without increasing the exterior diameter of the tube. Butting not only means less weight, it also allows the frame to absorb road shock better because of the flexibility of the tubes' center sections.

Until recently, all butted alloy tubing was seamless. It cost significantly more than seamed tubing, which had a reputation for low quality in its high-tensile steel form. However, seamed, butted chrome-moly tubing has been found to be almost a match in quality for its seamless cousin. Couple that fact with the much lower cost of seamed, butted chrome-moly tubing, and it becomes a bargain to watch for. Tube sets of this type include Tange 900 and 1000, Ishiwata EXO and EX. Columbus will soon offer one as well.

In the past, aluminum tubing was used only in very expensive framesets, but now Cannondale is making and marketing aluminum-frame bicycles that begin in price around $400. Oversize-tube aluminum frames, such as the Cannondale and the more expensive Klein, are stiffer and more responsive than many steel frames. Aluminum frames that utilize more normal tube

Photograph 2-1. The standard ATB on the market today combines the lightness of alloy rims and frame with the ruggedness of motorcycle style handlebars, cantilever brakes, and knobby tires.

diameters, such as the Vitus and Alan frames, are known more for their forgiving rides than their rigidity.

Wheels

Now that alloy rims are commonly found on bikes in the sub-$200 range, you are unlikely to have to choose between them and steel rims, but if you are confronted with the choice, go for the aluminum. Alloy rim wheels give far superior braking in wet weather, allow livelier riding because of their generally lighter weight, and (given current fabrication techniques) are almost as strong—in some cases stronger—than steel rim wheels.

Rims and tires for road bikes come in 27-inch and 700C sizes and in widths from a narrow 1 inch to a wide 1⅜ inches. By contrast, tires made for all-terrain bikes generally range in size from 26 × 1½ inches to 26 × 2⅛ inches. The wider tires are generally chosen for serious off-road riding and will float you over a lot of soft or wet surfaces that narrow tires would sink into. On the other hand, the smaller tires are zippier in the acceleration department. Here again, it helps to know your needs when making a selection.

Most ATB riders are best served by combination tread tires, which offer a raised ridge in the center of the tire. You can live with these tires on the street, and the traction tread on the sides of the tire will allow some extra traction off-road compared to standard street balloon tires. Use the super knobbies when you get serious about riding off the pavement.

An ATB Sampler

In preparation for *Bicycling*'s 1985 Buyer's Guide issue, members of the staff selected and tested four all-terrain bikes—the BCA Classic, Mongoose All-Terrain, KHS Montana, and the Takara Highlander. All four of these bikes come equipped with the elements needed to make a fun-to-ride ATB that weighs approximately 30 pounds: aluminum ballooner rims and lightweight ballooner tires, frames with the three main tubes made of at least straight-gauge chrome-moly steel, triple chainwheel, wide-range gearing, and an alloy component group.

Aluminum rims and lightweight tires are important because they reduce the bike's rotating weight (compared to steel rims and thick blackwall tires), allowing for quicker acceleration and more responsive handling. The test bikes all came with 26 × 2.125 tires, though within this size classification there is a wide variety of treads and profiles. For the bikes we tested, the manufacturers wisely chose not to use either all-out off-road "knobbies" or street-type treads but instead turned to mixed-tread tires.

Of course tires and wheels are only a part, albeit an important part, of the handling picture. If you're going to get the best performance from your ATB purchase, be sure to give serious consideration to sizing. A rule of thumb to follow is to select an ATB frame whose seat tube is two to three inches shorter than that on the frame of your 10-speed road bike. ATBs are more rewarding to ride when you can move your weight freely from front to back and side to side without banging a thigh on the top tube.

But make sure the overall frame fit is right, too, allowing stand-up riding without having your knees collide with the handlebars. Most dealers today are aware of the special sizing requirements of ATBs, so if you go to a competent dealer, you are not likely to be stuck with a size you'll be unhappy with later on.

Choice Features

Some features that our resident experts consider important to look for in an all-terrain bike are sealed or shielded bearings—for protection against the mud, dirt, and debris that are frequently encountered in off-road riding—and mixed-tread tires for good traction off the road and smooth running on pavement. Brakes should be the cantilever type. These are difficult to adjust but necessary for the fat tires. Other choice features are quick-release seats and chrome finish. The quick-release seat is important because of the varying seat heights needed for different

Photograph 2–2. Chrome finish, such as that on this Mongoose All-Terrain, made by BMX Products, is a good choice for a bike that is going to be subjected to rough, off-road use.

types of riding. The chrome finish is ideal because it will resist nicks and scratches far better than the best of paints.

Conclusion

The popularity of the all-terrain bike, in its various forms, appears to be increasing, rather than diminishing, which encourages manufacturers to take a more long-term view of this segment of the bike market. This works to the advantage of the prospective buyer of an ATB because it means prices will tend to decrease and features increase as competition in the market builds momentum. Already, bikes equipped with high-quality alloy frames featuring scads of brazed-on fittings, smoother and more reliable drivetrains, and better finishes are readily available.

So take a careful look around before you buy, whether you're looking for a whistle-wetter under $300 or a hand-finished beauty in the over $800 range. And remember, whether you're interested in an ATB that will take you as fast as your growing skill will allow off the road or a curb-hopping commuting bike that's at home on the back roads for weekend wandering, there's already something in the $300 to $400 price range that will appeal to you.

Selecting the Right Gearing for Your ATB

An off-road bike uses its fat knobby tires and ultra-long-wheelbase touring geometry to prevail over steep terrain and rough surfaces. It has equipment different from a road bike's so that it will have different capabilities. Even though the gearing looks like wide-range touring bike gearing, it has important differences.

The lowest gear on an ATB is lower than that on a road bike, so you can pedal (rather than push) up any hill that your rear wheel can grab. The gear train is also designed for quick, positive shifting under load. The steps between gears are wider so that when you shift one step, you feel a significant difference.

Off-road bikes use extra-long cranks to make possible a low-cadence, stand-up-and-stomp hill-climbing technique. Their components are sturdier so that they survive longer in the high-shock, wet, dirty, off-road environment. These are the general differences between ATBs and road bikes.

To some extent, the components that serve off-road needs best have been selected by trial and error. In the mid 1970s, the pioneer fat-tire riders in Marin County used hybrid mixtures of BMX, racing, and touring components in their gear trains. The Mount Tamalpais/Repack Road test laboratory (described in the first part of this book) quickly identified the weak parts, and the list of survivors spread by word of mouth.

Manufacturers who were largely unaware of the off-road market were sometimes caught by surprise when their products passed the test. For example, at one point Simplex-USA discovered they were selling four front derailleurs for every rear derailleur. The SLJA-523 front derailleur was an early survivor of off-road use.

Today, off-road bikes have every manufacturer's attention. Sakae Ringyo (SR), Shimano, Sugino, SunTour, and Takagi now provide partial or complete selections of factory-designed off-road equipment. What you want to know is how to select a component group that will tailor the gear train on your off-road bike to your specific riding needs. Of course, if you are buying a new bike, customizing the gearing will probably cost you more than simply taking it as is. Even so, familiarizing yourself with gearing options should help you make an intelligent choice when buying a bike off the rack in your local shop.

If you use your fat-tire bike mainly on paved roads, you'll probably be happiest with a conventional half-step-plus-granny touring gear train. This means using two chainwheels so nearly the same size that double shifting is necessary to move through gear sequences, plus a very small third chainwheel that provides an additional set of gears lower than the rest. There are zillions of possible half-step combinations, but one example of a good pavement/dirt hybrid is to use 26/43/48 chainrings with a 13–16–19–23–28 freewheel. But, since the real genius of the ATB is its off-road capability, our discussion will concentrate on gearing for riding on unpaved roads.

Choosing High Gear

High gear uses the big chainwheel and the little freewheel sprocket. The normal way to select your optimum high is to pick the wrong one (too high or not high enough) for your first gear train. You correct the mischoice the second or third time around. The normal way is also probably the best way, since no two mountaineers have the same strength or pedal over the same terrain. That said, here are some rough and ready rules.

High should be somewhere between 85 and 105 inches.

(The formula for calculating gear inches is to divide the number of teeth on the front sprocket or chainwheel by the number on the rear sprocket or freewheel cog, then multiply that number by the outside diameter of the rear wheel.) For most riders, the lower end of this range is plenty high enough. The highest two or three gears (for example, the big chainwheel gears) are mostly used on paved roads, getting to and from the trails. On level dirt, you won't use gears much above 60 inches. You also won't be pedaling downhill at 100 rpm and 35 mph on rough trails unless you own stock in an emergency hospital, so there's just not much reason to use high gears on an off-road bike.

The long (175- to 185-millimeter) cranks slow your cadence down a bit, which lets you use a higher gear. But this effect seems to be cancelled out by the higher wind resistance of the upright position and the slightly higher rolling resistance of fat tires.

Most bikes (ballooners as well as standard) use a 14-tooth freewheel sprocket (instead of a 13) to reduce chain load. You combine this with a big chainwheel in the 46- to 52-tooth range to get an 85- to 97-inch high. If you like bombing downhill on paved roads, you might want a high above 100 inches. The 13-tooth freewheel sprocket is a better route to a high gear than an oversize chainwheel because it keeps the front derailleur capacity within bounds.

Big chainwheels with fewer than 46 teeth may require you to mount the front derailleur too low. The heel of the front derailleur may foul the rear derailleur cable (if the cable is routed above the bottom bracket). So as you can see, these mechanical restrictions keep your big chainwheel within a narrow size range. It's a fortunate coincidence that the high gears come out right with commonly used (13-tooth and 14-tooth) small cogs.

Choosing Low Gear

Choosing low gear is fairly straightforward. The grades you'll encounter off the road are much steeper than those on pavement. You can't be too low when you're mountain climbing, and you can always use second gear. Install the smallest granny chainwheel that will fit your crankset. Combine this with a 34-tooth big freewheel sprocket. Low will be in the 19- to 22-inch range, depending on whether your crankset takes a 24-, 26-, or 28-tooth chainwheel.

If the crankset on your bike won't accept tiny chainwheels with fewer than 30 teeth, there is an alternative available. SunTour's AG rear derailleurs do a heroic job of shifting smoothly on the 38-tooth AG rear sprocket. This derailleur and huge cog will go a long way toward putting desirably low gears on your bike. Adding them is less expensive than buying a completely new high-quality touring crankset.

Gear Selection

By trial and error, off-road gearing has evolved into a pattern. You have three distinct gear ranges, one on each chainwheel. The big chainwheel is for street riding. The middle chainwheel is for level and uphill trails. The inner chainwheel is used only with the two or three big freewheel sprockets. These bull-low gears are used for belaying up near-vertical pitches. The chain will hang slack in the small chainwheel/small cog combination, and it's assumed you have the brains not to use them. Almost all shifts are made on the rear derailleur. No one bothers to coordinate the gears between chainwheels because there's no double shifting.

If you accept our proposal that all mountain freewheels should have a 14 to 34 spread, and you like relatively even steps between gears, then your five-cog freewheel should be 14–17–21–26–34, and your six-cog should be 14–17–20–24–28–34. This gives 25 percent steps and 20 percent steps between gears, respectively. You can move a tooth or two on these selections to suit your fancy.

Pick the middle chainwheel somewhere between 36 and 42 teeth to match your hills, your quadriceps, your crank length, and the bolt circle of your crankset (more on this later). Smaller middle chainwheels climb steeper hills and spin out earlier on level trails. If the middle chainwheel is too small, you may encounter front derailleur problems when you upshift from the granny. What happens is that a too-small middle chainwheel can hide in the shadow of the large chainwheel. When the front derailleur shoves the chain over, the chain never sees the middle chainwheel. But with some of the newer front derailleur designs, this won't be a problem.

Freewheel and Chain Selection

Shimano and SunTour make the freewheels of choice. No one else offers the large 32- and 34-tooth rear cogs. Shimano's Freehub, which is available in five, six, or seven speeds, with a number of different hub widths (over locknut spacing), raises lots of possibilities. Some of them aren't appropriate for off-road riding. The five-cog version with 124-millimeter over locknut spacing is the best choice; the five-cog 120-millimeter and six-cog 126-millimeter are in second and third places (if your frame can take a 120-millimeter spacing).

If you're using a conventional separate hub and freewheel combination, you can choose among five cogs, six cogs, normal spacing, and narrow spacing. Some of this will be dictated by the manufacturer of the bike. Some bikes come with 130-millimeter rear hub spacing, which moves the freewheel—and the chain—farther from the centerline of the bike. (This keeps the chain from scraping on the sidewall of that fat tire.) The manufacturer will also decide whether to leave room for a normal-width 6-speed freewheel. Don't rearrange the hub to cram one in. That would increase the rear wheel dish and decrease the wheel strength. You can always use a narrow 6-speed freewheel, which will give you narrower spacing among gears for street riding.

The Shimano Uniglide is one of the smoothest operating chains because of the wide spacing between its plates. However, since it is a wide chain, you can't use it with narrow freewheel spacing. The Sedisport and DID Lanier chains work with either narrow or wide-spaced freewheels and also have good reputations.

Cranksets

Here then are some of the features you should look for in a triple crankset for a mountain bike.

- 24-tooth minimum inner chainwheel
- 34-tooth minimum middle and outer chainwheels
- crank lengths from 165 to 185 millimeters
- close spacing between the middle and outer chainwheels, so the chain can't ride on top of the middle chainwheel
- a wide gap between the outer chainwheel and the crank-arm so you can use today's wide-cage front derailleurs

The Sugino Aero Tour is one example of a crankset with these characteristics. It has been such a success that Takagi and SR have produced almost exact copies.

Before Sugino came out with the Aero Tour, the T.A. Cyclotouriste was the most popular mountain crankset. It has both good and bad points. It can use a 26-tooth minimum chainwheel. It has the widest range of chainwheel sizes and crank lengths of any crankset, and it's been around for ages, so parts and chainwheels are widely available. These are points in its favor. The bad news is that the T.A. right crank is so close to the outer chainwheel that you have to use old-style narrow-cage front derailleurs. Also, the T.A. design allows crankarms and chain-rings to flex, which is bad news for strong pedalers.

The Stronglight 99, SR 5ATG, and Shimano Deore are 28-tooth minimum touring triples rather than real born-again mountain cranksets. They're all good, but none of them has all of the Sugino's off-road attributes. The smallest middle chainwheel for the Deore is a 39-tooth. And only Shimano's Deore pedals fit the DynaDrive special one-inch pedal thread, unless you use the adapter introduced by Shimano.

Stronglight has widened the gap between the crank and the chainwheel on current 99 production, so you can use any-one's front derailleur. The spacing between the outer and mid-dle chainrings of the Stronglight 99 and the similar SR 5ATG is a bit wide. This is more of a problem with half-step gearing than with typical off-road bike gearing.

If you wear Gucci cycling shoes and like to flaunt your bankroll, Wheelsmith or Gary Klein will drill and tap a Campagnolo double chainwheel for adding a 24-tooth inner chainwheel. You use Avocet bolts and studs. The finished product has the same problems as the Avocet: the 41- or 42-tooth middle chainwheel is too big for mountain service, and the crank-to-chainwheel gap is on the skimpy side.

Rear Derailleurs

The three new SunTour "Tech" rear derailleurs (Superbe Tech, MounTech, and AG Tech) plus the Huret Eco Duopar are the standout rear derailleurs for mountain bikes. They shift predictably and reliably over 14 to 34 freewheels and under load.

The wide-range SunTour GT rear derailleurs and the Shimano Deore XT are a small step down in shifting precision. The Deore XT includes Shimano's self-centering action. If you insist on really thrashing the bike around, the steel SunTours (such as the AG Tech) are probably the most rugged.

Front Derailleurs

Front derailleur performance has improved dramatically in the past five years. The better-performing new front derailleurs have a pronounced curve on the top of the inner cage to help lift the chain from the inner chainwheel.

On many of the new derailleurs, the cage is wider at the rear, which lets you make three or four rear shifts without fine-tuning the front derailleur. Finally, in the last few years, Simplex, Shimano, and SunTour have made mountain derailleurs with extra deep inner cages. They work especially well on mountain (26/38/50, for instance) chainwheels. They don't work well on half-step chainwheels (26/45/50, for example) because they have to be mounted too high to clear the middle chainwheel.

Some derailleurs are rigid, and some are flexible; and in this case flexibility is a demerit. If the cage bends on upshifts, then the chain wedges between the cage and the chainwheel, and you can't shift under load. Most of these comments apply equally to off-road bikes and wide-range touring bikes. The demands are the same. In fact, the tourist makes more shifts on the front derailleur than does an off-road rider.

The SunTour MounTech and AG Tech, and the Shimano Deore XT are probably the best mountain bike derailleurs available at present. All of these derailleurs need a wide gap between the crank and the chainwheel. If you don't have a wide-gap crankset, then you need a narrow-cage derailleur. The Simplex SLJA-523 and its siblings are the best of these. The Campagnolo Record is rigid, but it is limited to a chainwheel difference of about 18 teeth. The Huret Duopar and Success front derailleurs have lots of capacity, but they are on the flexible side.

Shift Levers

Ratchet-style, handlebar-mounted shift levers let you shift gears with your thumbs with both hands on the handlebars. SunTour's Mighty Shifter was the only model available until 1983. In fact, you could count off-road bike sales by counting Mighty Shifter sales and dividing by two. But since that time, several new models have appeared on the market. SunTour has come up with a sexy new Power Thumb Shifter, and Shimano has developed the very-well-thought-out Deore XT. Huret has also come out with a ratchet thumb shifter.

These observations having been offered, we hasten to point out that the bicycle component market changes rapidly, with new products appearing all the time. And given the current popularity of off-road bikes, manufacturers will increasingly turn their attention to producing products designed with the special needs of these bikes particularly in mind. Thus, by the time you read these recommendations, components will undoubtedly be available that are as good or better than those we have mentioned. This being the case, we advise you to use our examples as illustrations of the kinds of features you should look for when you set out shopping rather than as the final statement on the subject.

The City Bike Alternative

What's the perfect solution to the commuting blues? Riding a bicycle, natch. But what's the perfect commuting bicycle? What do you use to dodge potholes, skim skidlessly over manhole covers, crunch over broken glass with nary a puncture, evade taxi fenders, slalom through vendors' carts, track-stand motionlessly at stoplights, and gain a panoramic view of all these proceedings? The almost universal answer offered by the bike industry in 1984 was the *city bike*, an urbanized version of the mountain bike.

The all-terrain bicycle is a nearly perfect city warrior. It's agile, tough, comfortable, and lightweight. But for many riders, the full-fledged ATB is overkill for city use. The buzz of dirt-bred knobby tread against asphalt loses its novelty fairly quickly. Perfect mountain gearing is too wide-range and adds unnecessarily to a city bike's cost, and the long reach to the bars on some ATBs bunches your suit jacket up around your armpits—a valid complaint if you have to face it every morning on your commute to work.

The manufacturers of city bikes started with many design features found on the rugged all-terrain bike, then modified them for city use. The most obvious change is in the tires. The hard knobbies found on true off-road vehicles are exchanged for smoother treads and, in many cases, narrower profiles as well.

But city bike manufacturers have other tricks up their sleeves, too. For example, to deter theft, most (though not all) city bikes drop the quick-release seatposts commonly found on ATBs as well as the quick-release wheels common on racing bikes. (Nuts and bolts won't stop a kid with a Crescent wrench, but they'll slow down a casual seat nabber.) Toe clips and straps are avoided in favor of ATB-type platform pedals for quick city dabs (i.e., setting foot to pavement), and most of these pedals have flat surfaces instead of the gonzo, sneaker-grabbing pins that are so slippery on leather shoes.

The straight handlebars on an ATB allow for a relatively upright position on the bike, which is a great asset for city riding. You're not hunched over like you are when gripping the drops on a racing bike. Most of the new city bikes have a high-rise version of the ATB handlebar, which—especially when accom-

panied by a relatively short top tube—lets you sit very upright.
You cruise in comfort, controlling the bike with conveniently
placed thumb shifters and tourist brake levers, while getting a
good view of your surroundings. No longer are you craning
your neck around to the side to see. In fact, on a city bike, you
can often look over the traffic in front of you. Your suntan glows
on your forehead, where it belongs, instead of your neck, and
your glasses don't slip off when you power over trolley tracks.

Variety of Choices

One clear sign that city bikes are still a new phenomenon
is the lack of agreement on design among the manufacturers.
Apart from the fact that four of the five city bikes evaluated in
Bicycling's 1984 road test clearly evolved from ATBs, their
designs are quite divergent. What you find in this group are
5-, 10-, 12-, and 15-speed gearing schemes; cantilever as well as
sidepull brakes; and sprung mattress as well as racing saddles.
One has narrow handlebars and a medium-length top tube; another gives you plenty of breathing room thanks to a long top
tube and wide bars with a gentle rise. One is tall and stately,
while another is rugged and beefy. Two of the bikes have chainguards; one has fenders; one has a rack and a bell; one has front-
wheel retainers as theft deterrents; and one has Colorado-school
clunker frame geometry; but none has each of these things.

The positive aspect of this diversity in frames and equipment is that there is a good chance you will find a bike in this
category that you like. And the choice is not limited to the five
bikes we tested; other models are available as well. Most likely,
diversity will continue to be the name of the game in city bike
production for many years to come. So if you are in the market
for a city bike, don't rush out and buy the first one you see.
Look around; see what is available in your area. Test ride a few
models, and pick the one that is best suited to your long-term
needs.

Design Recommendations

Since the city bike is at this point much less of a clearly
defined entity than the racing bike or the touring bike—or even

its most immediate ancestor, the all-terrain bike—we can perhaps be permitted to indulge our fancies and suggest features that are missing from the models we have seen but strike us as logical for inclusion on the city bikes of the future. Possibly by the time you read this, some of these features will be found on bikes stocked in your local bike shops.

It seems to us that a major concern for anyone who uses a bicycle for commuting to work and shopping in the city is protecting that vehicle and its vital parts from being stolen. While nuts and bolts are a deterrent to thieves, the only effective way we know to keep what you own is to nail it down or lock it up. Therefore, it seems to us that the ideal city bike will be equipped with some kind of locking system. Antitheft axle and seat locks should be easy to adapt from their automotive equivalents.

City bikes could also come with a factory-mounted lock carrier. Sure, bolt-on brackets are available for most major bicycle U-locks, but wouldn't it be better to have a quick-release bracket for a lock brazed onto the bike's down tube at the factory? Such a bracket couldn't be stolen, nor would it work loose from vibration. And while thinking in that vein, how about a theft-proof tire pump mount? Failing that, telescoping pumps that ride in a detachable tool bag could be offered as a standard option.

Visibility is another major concern for the commuter, so we hope manufacturers of future city bikes will give more attention to making their vehicles visible at night than simply equipping them with a couple of reflectors. The first manufacturer to offer a foolproof—and theft-proof—lighting system, whether battery or generator powered, deserves much praise.

Even in this age when unprecedented numbers of North Americans are concerned with keeping fit and trim, few of us have changing facilities available to us at our places of work. So most of us who turn to bike commuting are forced to ride in our work clothes. Now no matter how much you love your bicycle, the old pant-leg chain stripe is a real bummer. Thus a chainguard should be a welcome piece of standard equipment on a city bike.

Granted, an enclosed chain and derailleur system requires some nonstandard parts and a dash of clever design, but at least one manufacturer has brought it off with mild success. Eliminating the derailleur system altogether opens the door to even more creative chainguards, such as the chain-enclosing tubing found on the Sterling Metro 5, one of the bikes in our test group.

Finally, weatherproofing is an important, if unexciting, matter that needs attention. City bikes get parked under downspouts or locked to light poles that sit next to the deepest puddle in the busiest bus lane in town. Corrosion must be thwarted. Stainless steel spokes, sealed hubs and bearings, cadmium-plated fasteners, and as many aluminum components as practicable would be a step in the right direction. Axle and cable grease fittings would add a splendid touch. And since bikes get ridden in rotten weather as well as parked in it, lightweight fenders are a necessity. Equally welcome would be some method of installing tire savers underneath the fenders.

Photograph 2–3. The Sterling Metro 5 adds the benefits of ATB technology, BMX innovation, and high-quality components to some features found on old English 3-speeds to produce the best city bike we have seen to date.

How Versatile Is the City Bike?

Since the origin of the city bike is so deeply rooted in the fat-tired clunker, you might ask whether these new brownstonemobiles might not be all-purpose bikes, too. After all, all-terrain bikes are supposed to go anywhere, so why not their city variants? Well, while true ATBs can function both on country roads and city streets, city bikes are happiest on pavement. The very items that civilize the city bike compromise its dirt-tracking ability. The ATB's fat tires, low gears, oversize tubing, and bar-stem handlebars (stem integrated into the bar, rather than separate) are there for a reason. Take those dirt-handling pieces away, and you've stripped the mountaineer of its soul.

Only one of the bikes in our test group could double as an on-road/off-road workhorse. It has an unsophisticated but beefy frame and mildly aggressive 1¾-inch tires. But though this bike has versatility, it was not considered by our testers to be the bike of choice for either rough, steep climbs or commuting. On any of the other city bikes in our test group, you'd be asking for trouble by exploring any wilderness beyond the neighborhood sandlot or an occasional gravel road.

So, if real rugged riding appeals to you, your best bet is to stick with a genuine ATB. But if getting around town in style and comfort is the name of your game, then you just might find a city bike out there tailor-made to fit your needs.

Part Three
Techniques for Riding over Rough Terrain

Climbing Techniques for Trail Riders

If you can't climb hills on an all-terrain bicycle, you might as well sell it and buy an old rowboat and a pair of rubber boots. If there's one thing you can't get away from in the course of off-road frolic, it is steep, bumpy, slippery hills. The worst thing about climbing hills off the road is not that the hills are there, but that your basic road-bike climbing technique and body position are next to useless.

Think about what you do when you climb a steep hill on pavement. You can run out of legs or lungs, but you very rarely run out of traction. The abundance of traction on the street has allowed all of us to develop a standing climbing technique that puts the body into a hips-forward, straight back position that enhances body strength. The steeper the hill, the more forward lean you naturally use, until, on very steep hills, you are so far forward that you can practice reading upside-down on your headtube emblem.

You may stretch your chain, torque your frame permanently out of alignment, or bend your cranks, but you will probably never spin your rear tire while climbing on a paved road. But now take your road bike to a steep dirt hill. Stand up and climb in the normal road-bike position, and ZIZZZ* ZIZZZ*WHUMP!—the bike suddenly loses traction, comes to an abrupt halt, and you are lying on your side. After an experience of this kind, you may well wonder how you are supposed to climb a hill off of paved roads.

On a long, not too steep, not too rough hill, you can and

should sit on the back of your seat and spin up in a low gear, just as you do on your road bike. The major challenges in seated climbing consist of steering around loose gravel and rocks and in keeping up enough speed to maintain your balance without veering alarmingly off cliffs and such.

This kind of seated climbing works well on smooth, firm hills and gravel roads, such as logging and fire roads, but is of limited use on trails. When a hill starts to get rough, with rock steps or roots or whatever, then seated climbing is no longer adequate. Unless all of your riding is done on surfaces as smooth as the top of a pool table, you will have to learn a new standing climbing technique.

When you are seated while climbing a hill, most or all of your body weight is concentrated on the rear wheel. Any time the rear wheel meets a sharp rise, the bike must lift that body weight very quickly, taking needed energy away from forward momentum. The bike resists this and will make every effort to stop instead.

But if you are standing when your wheel hits a sudden rise, you are able to shift your weight easily and swiftly forward just as the back wheel nears the obstacle, relieving the wheel of much of its vertical load and actually giving the bike extra forward impulse at just the right time. When you are standing on the pedals, your feet experience about 60 percent of the lift of the back wheel since the crank is roughly midway between the wheels. Your body, communicating with the rear wheel through the pedals rather than the seat, contributes less vertical inertia to the rear wheel.

New Tricks

Thus, if you want to scale difficult hills, you must stand up and pedal. But here's where things get a bit tricky. Getting a good grip with the rear wheel requires that you keep your body weight on it, yet when most riders stand up, their hips move forward and their center of gravity moves toward the front wheel. The unloaded back tire then spins, and all is lost. Shifting body weight back onto the rear wheel as you stand is the goal and can be achieved by adopting a new body position.

Photograph 3–1. When you stand up on your pedals, your body has a tendency to move forward, shifting too much weight off the back wheel, causing it to lose traction.

The pictures accompanying this chapter show the right way to stand and the wrong way. The correct way is simply to bend your arms at the elbows and lower your head, keeping your face roughly over the stem. Doing this causes your derriere to move rearward. Your center of gravity is now lower and farther

aft than it was in the road position, loading the rear wheel more
generously than before. Simply following the arms-bent, face-
over-the-stem rule makes a tremendous difference, and once
you master this technique, you will be able to ascend difficult
hills that would defeat you if you tried them sitting or standing
in the road-bike position.

Just as important as traction in climbing is maintaining
directional control. Strong muscles and good traction do you
no good if you repeatedly veer off into trees and chasms when
you attempt to climb. Well, there is a secret to steering on a
hill. The secret is to forget steering with your handlebars. Instead, steer by shifting your shoulders from side to side, letting
the natural stability of the bike's steering system cause the front
wheel to follow your shoulder's lead. Actually, this principle of
steering by shifting weight should be followed any time you are
trying to hold a line on rough terrain—up, down, or level.

Photograph 3–2. The correct way to climb is with your arms bent,
your face over the stem, and your rear end back so that your center
of gravity is low and plenty of weight rests on the back wheel for
good traction.

Getting the Right Equipment

There are many ways in which your equipment affects your climbing ability. The best rider in the universe won't get very far up a difficult hill on a bike that is poorly suited to climbing. The main problem that you run into with most off-the-shelf ATBs is that their chainstays are way too long. This pushes the rear wheel far enough back that no riding position will let you get traction while standing. The shorter you are, the more critical chainstay length becomes. If you are a short person and have a bike with 19-inch chainstays, you will have extreme difficulty ever getting traction while standing, and you will have to attempt all hills in the sitting position. This is a severe handicap. A six-foot-five football player might not have any problem climbing with the same machine, simply because his rear end extends back farther when he is in the proper climbing position.

The moral of this story is that if you are short, or even six feet tall, you will want to buy an ATB with a chainstay length of 17½ inches or less. Basically, the shorter the chainstays, the better a bike will climb once the rider is used to the greater sensitivity it affords. Our "rough stuff" expert, John Olsen, says he climbs best with a chainstay length of around 16½ inches. At that length, John's bike will stick on hills that he can hardly believe he's climbing.

Unfortunately for serious trail riders, few ATBs are designed with chainstays for these extremely steep climbs. (Instead, they usually have chainstays 18 or more inches long, which is good for high-speed descending and for touring with panniers.) If you want a bike like John Olsen's, you'll have to get it custom-made, as he did.

For serious climbing work, your bike should be equipped with knobby tires inflated only to around 15 psi. Obviously, the more aggressive the knob and the softer the rubber, the better the tire will stick to the hill. Of course when operating tires at pressures that low, you do run the risk of pinching the tube against the rim if you hit a rock on a descent. Also, you may get tire slippage, which will lead to tube failure at the stem. To prevent the latter problem, deflate the tire and brush a thin layer of rubber cement on both the inside of the rim and the tire rim bead. Let it dry, then inflate the tire and you will be able to travel without slippage.

When you need speed on a hill (which is virtually all the time), get it by spinning in a lower gear (say, 26 gear inches for starters) rather than by shifting into a higher gear. With a low gear, you *will* slip some every time, but with a high gear, once you lose speed, you are sunk. Any obstacle, looseness, or increase in steepness will require an anticipatory burst of speed, gained by a smooth increase in revs. Remember that inertia is your best friend on a challenging hill—lose speed and you are in trouble.

An attack on a difficult hill should be an intense, fluid, high-revving sprint, with head down, elbows bent, and derriere back. Any obstacles should be anticipated by accelerating. All steering should be led by the shoulders, and the upper body should constantly be working fore and aft, maintaining just the right weight split between the wheels.

You will find that climbing a nasty hill off the road is about 40 times more skill-intensive than riding up a paved hill. But once you've mastered the art—oh, my!—how you can amaze your friends!

The Safe Way to Descend Steep Places

What goes up eventually must come down! When it comes to climbing things like giant rocks, trees, and the roof of your house, going up may be exciting, but coming down is often frightening. The same can be true when you go climbing by bike. Oh sure, in one sense gravity makes it easy to descend a steep slope; you can simply sit back, hang on, and pray that you make it to the bottom in one piece. That's one way to descend, but not one we recommend; only good technique can make your steep descent a safe descent. So now that we have explained how you and your ATB can climb to the top of that steep hill, we better let our "rough stuff" expert, John Olsen, tell you the best way to get back on level ground again.

Swing Low, Sweet Fat-Tire Bike

I am fairly fond of my nose. Oh, sure, Robert Redford probably wouldn't want to wake up with it grafted onto his face one morning, but it has served *me* well. I breathe through it, I look down on it, and sometimes I land on it. It is, in fact, a sort of semihydraulic shock absorber for my face, a sacrificial damper, an interface between me and the forest floor, used whenever I push beyond the performance envelope in all-terrain-bike descents.

In spite of this constant cranial trauma, I really *like* to ride down steep, nasty descents, as long as I can do it slowly and in control. Many ATB riders haven't developed the skills necessary to overcome their initial fear of steep descents. It's a shame. With the right equipment and technique, very steep drops can be taken at a comfortably slow pace. With the wrong equipment or technique, well, better stay in the middle of a dry lake bed, okay?

I don't pretend to speak for the ATB cyclists who like steep descents at *high* speeds. Theirs is a different pleasure. And whatever the merits of the high-speed thrills I eschew, note that some of the same techniques I describe here are important for their descending, too. Also, I might add, slow speed makes it possible to safely descend slopes so steep that they lead expert high-speed riders to call for a helicopter rescue.

The two major descent situations are these: short, vertical or overhung descents (boulders, big logs, and large obstacles like junk cars) and long, sustained, steady-state descents. Both require the same equipment, but they differ considerably in technique.

In both cases, you need very good brakes and the ability to put your weight back and down. The brakes aren't much of a problem as long as they are dry. Good ATB cantilever brakes can handle most dry descents. The two big problems for most riders are getting their weight in the right place and using those good brakes well.

Equipment Factors

Proper weight distribution depends on two equipment factors: selecting the proper frame size and making good use of the quick-release seatpost. The sad fact is that most new ATB riders buy (or are sold) frames that are way too big for them to use safely in the dirt. You simply can't get your derriere back and down far enough for the steep descents that abound in off-road riding if you are riding a tall frame.

What is a tall frame? Consider my example. I have a 33-inch inseam, and I ride a 23-inch or 24-inch road or track bike. If I were to go and buy an ATB from the average bike shop, I'd probably be encouraged to buy the 21-inch size. An above-average shop would recognize that 21 inches is too large, and steer me toward the 19-inch size.

Most ATB enthusiasts would be satisfied by this, but in my book there's still room for improvement. My own ATBs (one is a Raven trials bike of my own design; the other is a stock Cannondale) have 14- to 15-inch seat tubes (measured center to center) and 28 inches overall top tube height. This gives me a safe 5-inch gap between top tube and groin when I straddle the bike.

In order to get this clearance, both bikes use slanted top tubes—a very good design feature. But most ATB manufacturers have stuck with traditional horizontal top tubes and lessened crotch clearance for two reasons: first, cyclists expect adult bikes to have horizontal top tubes and don't yet understand how a slanted top tube improves crotch clearance, and second, most component manufacturers do not yet build long enough seatposts to allow low enough top tubes.

When riding on difficult terrain, I leave my saddle down as far as it goes. I only raise it to a comfy sitting height when riding on smooth terrain (roads, smooth trails, long packed hills, grades gentle enough to permit me to ride in the saddle, etc.). As soon as I come to a challenging slope, down goes the saddle. Bless the person who invented the quick-release seatpost!

When my seat is all the way down, it is about 33 inches above the ground. I can straddle it when the bike is on level ground. You should be able to straddle your saddle, too, if you want to ride steep off-road terrain. You should also have a narrow saddle that will pass between your thighs easily when you scoot your rear end back. Wide women's saddles won't work.

Assuming, then, that your equipment is in order (small-frame ATB, good brakes, and a quick-release seatpost), here are some techniques for descents and drop-offs.

Back Is Beautiful

On a long, steep descent, you must control your speed from the very top. The best you can hope for on a difficult hill is to maintain a low speed; don't assume that you will be able to slow down once you have gained momentum. On a steep descent, virtually all weight is on the front wheel, and all braking is done by the front wheel. The back wheel is there mainly for steering and balance.

Your feet exert steering forces on the back wheel through the pedals. You never steer by turning the front wheel—the bars would be torn from your grip. You steer by shifting your weight and by pushing the back end of the bike around with your feet and your knees, which are resting against the sides of the saddle.

Your arms are bent, not straight and locked; all your weight is supported by your arms and shoulders. Your chest is down as low as comfortable, near the saddle, and your butt is way behind the saddle. Your butt is the counterweight that keeps you from landing on your nose.

You grasp the back brake lever lightly, with two fingers. The rear wheel is easily locked up with the brake, and the goal is to keep it *just* this side of skidding, except when you want it to slide during a steep turn. The front brake may need four or five of your most skilled and sensitive fingers. Because I am right-handed, I use my right hand for the front brake. If you don't already have your front/rear braking reflexes developed, you may wish to modify your brakes to do likewise. Conventional bike setup is apparently intended for lefties!

Photograph 3–3. When turning on a steep descent, keep your shoulders and handlebar pointed squarely downhill and steer by pushing the seat with your knees.

Turning on a steep descent can be done in several ways. My favorite flashy method is the rear-wheel-floating turn, in which one gives a little extra squeeze on the front brake and a hop on the pedals and a nudge on the saddle with the knees. The front wheel stays pointed down the hill until the turn is completed. This method requires skill, practice, and a good helmet. The back wheel should barely come off the ground. You are really just taking the weight off it, as you would in skiing. The whole motion is very similar to that required for a parallel turn with long skis—down, unweight, twist your torso, and land. It's pretty, and it's crowd-pleasing.

A less spectacular turn is the rear-brake turn. Lock the rear wheel, which greatly reduces its resistance to being pushed sideways, and use your knees and feet to push the rear end of the bike sideways. Get off the back brake when you don't want to turn any more.

Take care! If you take your feet off the pedals or sit on the saddle on a steep descent, your weight will be too far forward, and you will go over the handlebars. So practice the technique I just described on a user-friendly hill, and be brave. Keep your saddle down, your butt behind the saddle, and your feet on the pedals, or trauma will be yours.

Drop-off Technique

Coming off a drop-off is trickier. It may be short, but by definition it's vertical (or even undercut). It requires dynamics, strong shoulders and wrists, and a weak imagination. Here's how to get down safely:

- First, don't ride down into a landing area you haven't previously examined for wheel-grabbing pits or snags. Look before you flop.
- Second, keep a bit of momentum up. If you stop at the edge and put your feet down, you won't make it. Go too slowly, and your front wheel will flop sideways.
- Third, don't go down slowly at all if the drop-off is higher than about 30 inches, consider leaping off. For this, you need a good place to land and a good run-up to build sufficient speed.

If it is safe to ride down slowly, ease up to the edge with the brakes on fairly firmly and the pedals horizontal. As the front wheel eases off the edge, pretend that your shoulders and head have stopped moving while the rest of you continues to move with the bike. Your hands move away from you as your arms straighten, and you automatically assume the butt-back, head-down, arms-out descending position.

The front brake stays on firmly until the front wheel is just about to hit the ground, then you let it off for a brief interval. As soon as the rear wheel starts to drop off the edge, you get back on the front brake to ease the rear end down. The rear brake stays on lightly throughout the descent.

Photograph 3–4. When heading over a steep drop-off, keep your pedals even, thrust your body as far back as possible, and use your front brake firmly while each wheel hits the ground in turn.

Your arms must stay strong but not locked, resisting the tendency of the front wheel to flop. It will want to flop as it rolls off the edge and again as it hits the ground with the bike tipped way up. As the rear end starts to ease down, your body moves forward again, ending in a normal standing position.

When I ride over my favorite "will I make it?" big log, my saddle hits my breastbone as I go down the other side. If my saddle or top tube were two inches higher, I would go over the bars on this log.

Be careful with sharp-edged vertical drops—most relatively low-slung ATBs (with 12-inch bottom bracket heights) will hit their chainwheels on a sharp edge, tipping you off balance. Rounded drop-offs are much easier on you and your chainrings.

So have fun and don't be terrified of down-hills and drop-offs. Wear a helmet and safety glasses, and begin by practicing these techniques on easy hills and logs. And don't mess up your nose!

Riding over Logs and Other Large Objects

Now that John Olsen has explained to you the basic principles for climbing and descending steep slopes, we will pass along his description of how to put these skills together in riding up and over big logs and other fun obstacles you may meet while riding your all-terrain bike.

Why Go Around, When You Can Go Over?

I suppose that sometimes there are a few reasons for riding your bike around logs. But for now, I want to teach you to look at logs with different eyes. A pleasant three-foot log, nicely shaped, with level ground on both sides—how could anyone turn it down? Yet, I've actually seen people stop and lift their bikes over such prime recreational logs. Once, I even saw a group of good off-road racers in California ride right by a perfectly good phone pole without stopping to play on it!

It's time for me to end this wasteful behavior by illustrating the techniques involved in riding over logs, rocks, and other large objects. For simplicity's sake, I'll refer only to logs, but the techniques apply to all large objects.

It's easier than it sounds. Briefly, you pick up your front wheel just in time to place it neatly on top of the log. Then you produce a tremendous leap in which you bounce the back wheel off the ground while simultaneously twisting wrists up on the handgrips, lofting the rear wheel right up the face of the log.

The accompanying photo sequence illustrates the basic steps involved in large obstacle crossing. Here are the technical details.

In photograph 3–5, I have just carefully and gently set my front wheel down on the top of the log. Notice that the soft front tire (15 psi) has just started to take weight, and my body is bent, ready to spring. My crank is almost horizontal, and I have stopped pedaling. From here on, all motive power will come from jumping, not from pedaling. But note that you need little forward speed to cross a log; the log in these pictures has a clear run-up of only about ten feet, enough room for only about 1½ crank revolutions in my 26-inch gear.

Then the jump begins. My shoulders and legs straighten explosively, compressing the back tire almost flat. The tire rebounds like a bouncing ball as my body continues moving upwards, and the bike floats up after me. The back tire of the bike leaves the ground, moving vertically about two inches away from the face of the log.

What goes up must come down—in this case, on top of the log. Photograph 3–6 illustrates my landing position. My feet have continued to come up after my shoulders have stopped rising. This allows the bike to come up higher onto the log because I am not hindering its motion. However, if I just froze in this position, I would probably not make it over the crest of the log. So I thrust the bike forward and up with my arms, using the inertia of my body to propel the machine over the last

Photograph 3–5. John Olsen begins his log jump by picking up his front wheel and placing it on top of the log.

Photograph 3–6. After pushing down hard against the rear tire of the bike, Olsen pulls his feet up, allowing the rear of the bike to rebound up onto the log.

Photograph 3–7. Olsen first pushes hard against the bars, then moves his body slightly forward to propel the bike over the far side of the log.

critical rise. In doing this, my body moves very far back over the rear wheel of the bike and my knees almost touch my chest.

This rearward body position is fortuitous, because now I face the most exciting part of the voyage—the descent. In the final photo, I have scooched forward on the bike just a bit, to make sure that it is going to continue forward, but my derriere is still well back. Note that I am making a steering correction by shifting my shoulder weight, not by turning the handlebars. If you are so foolish as to turn the bars while on a log, the wheel will keep right on turning, possibly taking the bars out of your hands, and certainly ruining the descent.

As I reach the bottom of my descent, my center of gravity is comfortably far back (slightly more so than is shown in the last photo) and my handlebars are straight, ensuring a safe landing. (If, at this point, I felt that I were in danger of going over the bars, I would be starting to bring my feet up and over the handlebars between my arms. That way, I would land on my feet and preserve my face.) At this point I also apply my brakes. This is to prevent the bike from picking up too much speed in the descent. This log crossing ends in a dry stream bed, and I have only about six feet in which to stop before making a very tight and strictly enforced turn!

If you want to ride over big logs, you will need a good helmet, gloves, knee and shin pads—for obvious reasons. It also helps to have an all-terrain bike designed for observed trials, with a short wheelbase, high bottom bracket, and very small chainwheel (26 or 28 teeth). If your ATB has larger chainrings, take them off before you go log-crossing. You'll just wreck them if you leave them on the bike. Photograph 3–5 makes it obvious that you don't want handlebars that are very high; nor do you want a very short stem.

With a properly equipped bike, you are ready to start jumping. Just remember: all-terrain bikes weren't invented to go around logs! So take the high road, not the long road. Today, a log; tomorrow, your new Corvette!

Riding in Snow

The advent of the all-terrain bike has brought about a new cycling activity—snow riding. But every activity has its special challenges, and for this one it is coping with ice. Any cyclist who has enjoyed a crisp, sunny winter day, only to turn head over heels on an ice patch, has longed for some extra piece of equipment. Tire chains maybe? Well, chains for bicycle tires have been invented and may be on the market by the time you read this, but some riders prefer to perfect snow-riding techniques that work well without chains. What follows is an account of the snow-riding experiences of a couple of adventuresome Coloradans.

Taking to the Slopes on an ATB

Kent Eriksen has paused at the top of a steep pitch, standing in silhouette, the morning sun behind him. Spring has come to the back country, bringing those magical times when a body can strike out over the still-frozen snowpack and go forever. The hour is early yet, but he has already covered miles of terrain in the mountains behind Steamboat Springs, Colorado.

This is Eriksen's turf; his cabin is in a neighboring drainage to the west. He is maybe three miles from the nearest plowed road and another three or four from the nearest paved road in Steamboat. The few folks who live back here either ride snowmobiles or ski in from the road.

Eriksen is an avid skier and a good one, but it is not skis that have carried him up into the back country this morning. He rode in over the snow on his all-terrain bike, and he intends to ride it down the pitch below him.

The pitch is short, perhaps 20 yards long from top to bottom. But it is steep enough to yield a strong adrenaline rush, and it bottoms out into a streamlet, exposed by the spring sun and running high and cold with snowmelt. He figures to try to take it head-on at the top, make a few traverse ski turns, and then pull out to the right in a long traverse that will ease him down next to the stream where it is spanned by a fallen tree.

He sits way back off the edge of his seat, his legs bent, feet squarely on the pedals, and rolls into what must look like a chasm to him. He gathers speed immediately, rolling down the frozen white hill, and actually executes a controlled turn or three. He looks pretty good, as if he might make it. But after the last turn, the descent becomes a free-fall-with-bicycle; he spins like an upsidedown turtle and careens into the fallen tree in the watercourse in an explosion of dead branches.

Bicyclists Who Adapt to Their Environment

According to the principle of natural selection, the cornerstone of the evolutionary process, a species adapts to the dictates of the environment. In the Colorado high country, snow dominates the landscape six to eight months a year. Most bicyclists simply pack it in with the first accumulations of snow in the late fall. But there are those—like Eriksen and Eric Sampson of Boulder—who have adapted to riding in snow.

Both Eriksen and Sampson manufacture all-terrain bikes: Moots and Rock Creek respectively. The bikes they make are constructed specifically—each to its designer's personal preferences—to deliver optimal performance in the rocky mountain environment. Both are zealots who ride year round.

Eriksen rides up the cross-country tracks and footpath that pass his cabin en route to the Steamboat Hot Springs. He has mounted a ski rack on the rear of his frame, and when the snow is too deep or soft to ride on or through (deeper than about four inches), he locks his bike to the nearest tree and continues on skis.

Sampson used to ride 15 miles each way on his commute into Boulder. He usually found this commute enjoyable, if a bit chilly. Occasionally, the freeze and thaw that accompany any snowfall on an eastern slope produced slush, and overnight, the slush would freeze into a solid slush pack full of frozen ruts. Slush pack can be formidable for even the best riders. So Eric invented a set of chains for his bike. And they work.

Asked to describe the special techniques for cycling in snow, both cyclists agree that the question is too broad.

"You have to get over calling it 'snow,'" Sampson says. "You have to think like an Eskimo. Don't lump all snow together. There are different kinds of materials that can behave differently. One of the most pleasant things I know of is to ride in three inches of light fluffy snow on dry frozen ground. It's so quiet—you can't even hear your chain."

Indeed, that's the kind of riding Sampson's colleague, Eriksen, usually sees in his rural surroundings. Eriksen doesn't own or use tire chains in Steamboat Springs; he used to use homemade bicycle tire studs when he lived in Wisconsin, but the cold, dry Colorado snow gives enough grip to make them unnecessary most of the time.

Eriksen offers no particular pointers for off-road riding without chains. "It's all reflex and balance," he says. It is a riding style that defies precise verbal description; though it is one that demands constant attention from the rider. Although he doesn't use them, Eriksen admits that some snow demands chains, and there are days when he wishes he had them.

Photograph 3–8. Riding in a few inches of light, fluffy snow can be a delightful experience, while riding on ice takes a lot of skill and concentration.

Chain Design

Sampson, the chain man, has devised a simple chain design with a quick-release feature that lets you get the chains on or off the bike in a minute or two. The chains have a "rope ladder" configuration like auto tire chains, with two large loops—one along each sidewall—and 18 crosswise chains bridging across the tread from one loop to the other. The quick-release is a little spring clip, the two loops are stainless steel cable, and the chains themselves are flat-link chain like you see on a dog's choke collar.

A bike with chains is not a high-speed rig. Sampson says he rarely uses a gear bigger than 65 inches or so, and a 40-inch gear is often tall enough for thick, wet snow. A snappy 80- to 90-rpm cadence is ideal, "but letting it fall to 60 doesn't hurt," Sampson says. "But if you're spinning slower than that, then you don't have the power if you hit a firm spot or scoop snow unexpectedly."

When the snow is deep enough that your feet scoop into it, a slower cadence (say, 40 to 50 rpm) helps: "It makes it more of a step onto the snow and less of a scoop through the snow," explains Sampson. But on ice, the old rules about cadence and spin go out the window. It's important to be absolutely smooth, with a perfectly even power stroke. Your cadence may drop to 40 rpm, and you still won't have use for a gear higher than around 60 inches.

A conversation with Sampson about winter bike handling can be intimidating. You sense you're talking to a real die-hard expert snow rider. For starters, Sampson prefers to put chains only on his rear wheel. He doesn't want them on the front wheel; he's greedy for traction but not worried about losing his steering on ice. Should the front wheel slide sideways, say, down into a frozen slush rut, Sampson says he relies on his own sense of balance so that he is once again balanced on top of the newly relocated bike. Not every bike rider is so nimble.

"We've ridden ice sheets on creeks," Sampson said. "If you pay attention to your center of gravity, and to the evenness of the torque you put on the pedals, you can ride the ice. Once in a while, you do go down. Ice is smooth and slick, which I can handle, but it isn't always flat—and when it slopes, your front wheel slides right out. You have to be loose on the bike. You can't ride ice if you're tight."

For a rider of lesser skill to lose the fear of falling on ice, Sampson agrees that "traction devices on both wheels" are desirable. But, he says, "it's a disaster to expect total security from them." Braking remains tricky. The tire will skid on the ice if you're "between chains," and you have to use finesse to brake safely. The state of the art in tire chains still calls for rider skill.

Many riders have tried studs instead of chains. Studs bite into ice nicely, but they ruin inner tubes, can't be removed quickly when dry pavement beckons, and don't necessarily grip well on wet concrete. Clearly, the perfect system has yet to be invented.

But as serious all-terrain bike builders ponder the question, better solutions will emerge. Eriksen and Sampson are two builders who have already proved their ability to solve problems; Eriksen makes his bikes quite versatile by offering a cantilever brake with movable mounting studs to accommodate a range of wheel sizes, and Sampson was the first on the block with an 11-inch, 14/34 gear for ultra-steep hills.

As more of this ingenuity is applied to snow, we may one day see a bike that will move comfortably over hard snow and even pavement. For all mountain dwellers who wish to adapt, such a bike would be a natural selection.

Part Four
All-Terrain Racing and Touring

Off-Road Racing Is Fun for Everyone

Off-road bicycle racing has arrived and not just on the West Coast, even though it may be better established there than elsewhere. If there aren't any special events for the fat-of-tire and young-at-heart in your area already, there probably will be soon. So get ready to have youself some fun.

Maybe you've never raced a skinny-tire bike and don't yet own a fat-tire bike, so you really can't imagine yourself getting involved in off-road racing. But the truth of the matter is, off-road racing differs greatly from its asphalt-coated cousin, and the differences allow for a greater range of participants, equipment, and more rider fun per mile in off-road events. So do yourself a favor and investigate the pleasures of this type of racing.

The major difference between ordinary road racing and the new off-road variety is that an off-road racer is primarily racing against the course rather than the other riders in a pack. Most traditional bicycle racing, except for time trials, cyclo-cross, and certain track events, revolves around the unity of the peleton. If you don't finish with the pack or in front of it, you are off the back and chasing. For most, the race is over then. By contrast, an off-road racer who knows that all the potential winners are up the road and—barring trolls—out of reach, can still have a ball just dealing with the course.

The downhill, high-speed portions are their own rewards. Descending on asphalt is a gas, too, but it's different. In a paved corner, you've either got traction or you've got serious trouble.

71

In the dirt, there is such a thing as partial traction. That, combined with the many opportunities to "get air" under your wheels,
gives an experience that feels like skiing. Many point-to-point
off-road races are weighted in favor of the descents by virtue
of an overall elevation loss, so the rewards are plentiful for the
climbing time.

The climbing, combined with the technical aspects of the
course, causes any semblance of a pack to disappear early in
most off-road races. So the experts can enjoy the downhills
without being surrounded by inexperienced hackers, and the
inexperienced get to try their skill at some very interesting bike
handling without having to worry about the traffic. Of course,
these races can be anything that a promoter might dream up,
but most race organizers wisely schedule some nasty hills or
some testy rocks, branches, logs, leaves, mud, water, and bogs
early in the race. These "hazards" are what is meant when it is
said that the riding in a certain zone is "technical."

Photograph 4–1. The abundance of "technical factors" in most off-
road races causes any semblance of a pack to quickly disappear.

Any Two Wheels Will Do

These races are open to any kind of human-powered unit you think will go the distance. Or as they say on grudge night at the drag strip, "Run watcha brung." If you have a nice old beater 10-speed and consider yourself at all deft in handling it, you might just enjoy an off-road race. The range of equipment we've seen pounding the dirt runs from 20-inch BMXers of one to many speeds, 26-inch ballooners packing from 1 to 21 speeds— including a tandem—plus a cyclo-cross bike or two and, on a relatively smooth course, even a road racing machine with heavy wheels.

Stay Loose

You'd like a few handling tips for the varied terrain out there? Okay, the first one is basic to all riding: stay loose. The more you can relax with arms and legs bent, the better off you'll be. Let the bike flap around underneath you, knowing that you carry the majority of the mass of your rolling unit in your torso. It's all right if the bike bounces around if you maintain your calm and let your limbs absorb the shock. Most of the time you'll be able to get that bike back to doing what it should before things get serious.

If a hole or a bump sneaks up on you while you're on the saddle and transfers the shock to your torso, roll with the punches: let that jolt stand you up, then deal with the bike. You can transfer the momentum of your body, once it has reached the top of its arc, into picking the bike out of any trouble it might have gotten into after the jolt and putting it back where you want it. If your paved roads are in as bad shape as the ones the editors of *Bicycling* usually ride on, but you like to descend fast anyway, you may already be a decent off-road rider and not yet realize it.

On very steep descents or any time you see a corner coming up too quickly, get your butt as far back and as low as possible. This will increase your braking power and improve your weight distribution for the turn. Once into the turn, let go of the brakes, as the wheels work much better for cornering traction when they're not trying to brake at the same time. If you're still going too fast or just can't handle it, use the rear brake and get that inside foot ready to plant in the classic three-point flat-track stance. This maneuver should slow you enough and get you around the corner, but beware: you may keep right on sliding until you're faced in the wrong direction, doing splits, on the ground, or all three. Be ready to let go of that brake.

If you're going fast and some nasty looking obstacles pop up in your path, sometimes you're better off in the air—it's much smoother up there. If you haven't learned to "bunny hop" it yet, don't worry. If you pull the front wheel up, the rear will follow when it whacks whatever it is you're trying to jump.

On the slow side of the hill, a large part of handling relies on the speed you can maintain, which relies on your level of fitness. When you edge up a hill in your wall-climbing gear, it takes a lot more skill to get you over and around the stuff that you could breeze through with a couple more miles per hour worth of momentum. But you won't be able to turn that higher gear forever, so you'll wind up at times with your tongue hanging out, picking your way through the technical stuff.

To get traction, you need to stay back on the bike, and to get power, you need to be up on the pedals. Since these are contradictory moves, that's where the quick-release seatpost is handy—to jack your saddle up in the air. But if you're really trying to make time in a race, you can't be stopping to adjust the saddle height at every hill, so it's helpful to develop the technique of standing up and back at the same time, and making the transition smooth enough that the action doesn't break traction.

To pick your way over rocks and logs at low speeds, pull up on the bars to get the front wheel over, then rock forward on the bike to unweight the rear wheel and get it up and over. This is like a slo-mo bunny hop that may never leave the ground.

When blasting through creeks, puddles, mud holes, or sand, if they look long enough to chew up most of your momentum, remember to shift down before you slow down, or you'll be stuck in a too-tall gear. Also remember that these kinds of terrains will slow you down much quicker than air!

Photograph 4–2. The Paradise Divide stage race combines challenging terrain with splendid scenery.

Anyway you handle it, these races shouldn't be missed—even if you have to borrow a BMX machine from your newskid. Beyond that, you'll need enough endurance to move the bike for two or three hours at a whack—an item some youngsters forget who are used to thinking in terms of one-minute motos. For us older kids, most promoters seem to have a way of showing up at the finish line with a keg or two as a solvent for the dust.

NORBA

As more and more competitive events for off-road bikes are being staged, race promoters frequently have difficulty gaining access to public lands. Government restrictions are primarily based on concerns about sharing trail use with folks on foot and horseback and concerns about the environmental impact of the vehicles. Sometimes lack of sufficient insurance coverage has been the stated reason for denial of use of public properties.

In response to these problems, the National Off-Road Bicycle Association (NORBA) came into being in 1983. The announced purposes of the association include lobbying for access to public lands and providing a sanctioning body for off-road racing to make insurance coverage easier and less expensive to acquire. Also, NORBA is initiating environmental research that compares the impact of fat knobbies to horse hooves and wafflestompers, negotiating with the governmental agencies that control land use, and contributing to the maintenance of trails used by bicyclists.

On the other side of the coin, NORBA encourages the responsible use of off-road bikes among its membership and anyone else who will listen. NORBA also intends to promote off-the-asphalt touring and recreational riding by providing its membership access to its files concerning where they may legally ride, as well as sanctioning tours and fun rides.

In short, NORBA is attempting to cover all the situations requiring organizational backing that concern anyone who heads her or his bike away from the network of paved roads in this country. Funding started on a grass roots basis through memberships at $15 annually. In return, riders are covered by a $10,000 accident insurance policy during NORBA sanctioned tours and races. They also receive a monthly newsletter that includes an events calendar and features about off-road riding, according to Glen Odell, president of NORBA.

The organization has attracted dealer, industry, and sustaining memberships as its momentum builds, complementing the growing list of individual members who wish to stay informed and have a voice. For more information and membership forms, send a self-addressed, stamped envelope to: NORBA, 2175 Holly Lane, Solvang, CA 93463.

Observed Trials for Bicyclists

Inevitably, when two off-road cyclists of a sporting turn of mind go riding together, the old "I bet I can get over that nasty looking rock" contest will begin. Well, what if we were to formalize this and invent a contest not of speed but of mobility, in which the winner was the rider who could pedal through the most challenging chunks of terrain and yet remain under control?

Although the concept is fresh to bicycling, contests like this are old hat to our motorcycle brethren. For years, British motorcyclists who did not care for pure speed have engaged in an off-road sport called observed trials. Specially marked sections of a closed course test the rider and machine against typical trail obstacles. Since agility and control are more essential than sheer power (because no high speeds are involved), the motorcycles used evolved from slightly modified street machines into extremely specialized, ultralight, fragile-looking things, with large, soft tires, high ground clearance, softly tuned, tractable engines with small carburetors and large flywheels, and very quiet exhausts.

The sport spread to the Continent and to the United States and has attracted a dedicated following of quiet individuals who are content to be away from the noisy high-buck mainstream of dirt motorcycling. In the past five years, bicyclists have joined in the fun, and there are now hotbeds of bicycle observed trials in Europe, Texas, California, and the Northwest. Soon this embryonic sport will blossom everywhere and will be found thriving in a gravel pit near you.

Keep Your Feet Up

Trialing is nothing more than the sport of looking for the hardest part of the trail and then riding through without putting your feet down. It's an absolutely natural application for all-terrain bikes. When an off-road biker rides a trail and comes to an obstacle and tries to get over it without (ugh) dismounting and carrying the bike across, then that rider is essentially practicing for his or her first trials competition. And really, the whole point of an all-terrain bike—or any bike for that matter—is to ride, not push or carry the bike.

Most bicycle trialing has been done on 20-inch-wheel BMX-type bikes. However, these small wheels suffer in soft terrain, tripping easily on small roots and rocks. While they excel at performing aerobatics, they are too small and nervous to climb sustained steep hills well. A special trials derivative of the 26-inch-wheel all-terrain bike, however, doesn't suffer from the small-wheel blues. In fact, a good rider can easily ride the same natural terrain sections as novice motorcycle trials riders and can even give the "engine guys" a hard time in many sections.

Trialing is more fun than shooting rubber bands at the back of your boss's head and less expensive in the long run. We can do it with slight modifications of our present all-terrain bikes and have a great workout while getting positively filthy. Clearly, the sport could not come more highly recommended.

How It All Works

An observed trials is a bit like a golf match in that the participants are encouraged to score as few points as possible. In trials, the rider who touches foot to ground the least often in the observed sections wins.

A trials course consists of perhaps ten sections, ridden in order for (typically) three laps. Plastic ribbon bits establish the boundaries within each section, red ribbon on the right and blue ribbon on the left. Paper plates attached to trees or other upright objects mark the beginning and end of each section; the plate at the beginning also displays the section number.

The rider is in the section when his or her front axle breaks the vertical plane formed by the "start" plate and the ribbon on the other side of the section. Safety is reached when the axle breaks the plane defined by the "end" plate and its opposite ribbon. Sections may vary in length but should incorporate terrain that is challenging enough that only the best riders can get through without setting foot to earth—or, in the vernacular, without "dabbing."

Riders can't practice the sections before the event begins,

so every section is a fresh challenge on the first lap. They can, however, walk through the sections, looking for the best line through whatever mess the organizers have thoughtfully laid out. Sections are ridden one rider at a time, so each rider can watch others go through, often learning how not to do it by direct example. Each section has an observer who watches to see that the rider stays inbounds and who counts the number of dabs made. When the rider finishes the section, the observer marks the rider's scorecard, usually by punching it with a paper punch.

The scoring system works like this. If the rider keeps his feet up through the section and doesn't go out of bounds, he gets a "clean" score of zero points. If he dabs once, he gets one point. If he dabs twice, he gets two points, and three dabs net three points. But just when the logic of the scheme seems unassailable, the scoring plan changes somewhat in that any further number of dabs still yields only three total points, as long as the rider doesn't have both feet on the ground at one time. However, crashing, going out of bounds, pushing the bike with both feet simultaneously on terra firma, coming to a complete stop in the section and putting a foot down, or otherwise propping up the bike results in a special five-point penalty. This is the maximum point yield for a section—five big ones.

So, for example, if you had three laps of ten sections each, the best score you could get would be no points at all, and the worst would be 5 × 3 × 10 or 150. A well laid out trial might take 30 points from the best rider and perhaps 120 from the worst, depending on the spread in rider abilities. A winning score of over 100 would imply that the trial was too difficult.

The trail between sections (called a "loop") can also form part of the challenge in that it may be tiring simply to ride from one section to the next. In general, bicycle trials loops should be kept short—less than a mile on flat ground, since the riders will get a good workout from the sections alone. Eventually, championship events might have longer loops, which would give the best athletes the advantage. Most trials events have a set time limit for completing the course.

Anything available within your local riding area can be used as obstacles in the sections. Tight turns are good for neophytes, as are small logs, rocky washes, long twisting climbs, very sharp

Photograph 4–3. Putting foot to ground and shoulder to tree after coming to a complete halt results in a five-point penalty for the section.

turns with obstacles in the way, abandoned VW Beetles—the list of ingredients is endless. The layout of a trials section is, in fact, limited only by common sense, safety, and the absolute requirement not to damage the environment. Go around ferns, not through them, and don't send riders up or down salmon streams during spawning season, for example. Finally, the person who lays out a section should ensure that it is ridable by either riding it himself or getting someone else to ride it.

Inside View of a Trials Section

So, you ask, what might an actual trials section look like? Let's walk through one and see for ourselves.

Imagine yourself deep in the woods on a low ridge. The ground consists of pine needles, gravel, and humus, making a kind of fiber-reinforced mud. The nearest fir tree bears a paper plate reading "Section One—Novice, Beginner—Begin." Five feet to the left, two chunks of blue surveyor's tape hang from a stick poked into the ground. From this starting line on top of the ridge, the section leads you down to a right turn onto the slippery slope of the ridge. Paralleling the ridge for 20 feet, you follow the red and blue markers to a tight, uphill, 180-degree turn on soft loam that leads you back toward the start.

Before you get to the start, the markers force you up the slope some more, and as you near the level ground top, the slope becomes greater, leaving you with an angled climb up the bank over exposed roots. Upon reaching level ground, the section turns tightly left, and you double back again, through a circle of rocks marking an old campfire. A tight right turn takes you up the steep shoulder of a small rise, squeezing you between the rise and two large cedar trees. After the last of these trees, you cut right and descend five feet to the "section end" pie plate and flag.

After walking the section, you watch with great interest as other riders try their luck, and you notice that all are having to dab as they lose momentum on that steep, climbing turn and don't have the traction to get going again. When your turn to ride comes, you line your bike up ten feet away from the entrance. Standing on the pedals with knees, arms, and back flexed, you balance for a moment of intense concentration, then smoothly pedal into the section, always standing. Pedaling against the resistance of your front brake, you creep down the side of the ridge and lean out and forward as you ease around the right-hander, pressing the front tire firmly into the pine needles.

Continuing to lean slightly away from the hill, you come to the dreaded turn. You pedal beyond the point at which the others have tried to turn up into the hill, riding to an area where the soil is still undisturbed. Stopping, you flex your arms and knees, spring back, and pivot the bike on its rear wheel, then bounce again and again until you are nicely lined up for the off-camber climb over the roots to the level. With good traction under your rear wheel, you accelerate strongly up the hill, flowing like a centipede over the slippery roots with all the momentum you have gained.

You let the last of the slope slow you for the left turn onto the rocks, swinging wide to get onto a good line. Approaching the campfire rocks now, you loft the front wheel and take one last pedal stroke, ending with the pedals horizontal, and bounce the front wheel off the top of the stable-looking rock you have chosen to kiss so sweetly. Your chainring clears the rock as you give a mighty bounce to the rear wheel and shift your weight forward. The back end comes up as the front comes down, and you have no time at all to prepare for the rocks on the other side of the little ring.

As soon as the back wheel returns to earth, you heave desperately on the bars and just clear the next rock, wobbling dramatically. Regrettably, you haven't the time to just bobble along all morning, and the right turn going up above the cedars has just gone by. Stopping briskly, you execute another bounce turn, throwing in some "back-up" for good measure, which lines you up for the climb. You have no speed, and your front wheel is on the rise, but you squat and put your shoulders into it and muscle your way past the trees, barely maintaining steerage way on the slippery surface.

Passing the second cedar, you fall out through the exit, waiting to make the crash official until the front axle passes the marker. As it does so, you relinquish all claim to equilibrium and topple gracefully into a clump of ferns. The observer shouts, "Clean! Nice exit, Jack!" as you lay on your back reflecting on how nice ferns look from underneath. Trials can bring you closer to nature.

Where to Find a Trials

Motorcycle trials clubs exist all over the country and can be found by asking any local motorcycle dealer. These clubs will probably welcome bicyclists, and most are eager to set up sections for you and watch you ride. In areas where the sport is more established, such as the Northwest, separate bicycle trials clubs exist, and these clubs usually put up posters in bicycle shops advertising events. This sport is in its infancy, and you may find yourself to be the first bicycle trials rider in your area. Just set up your own sections and show your friends, and soon you may be the organizer of the sport in your locale. Remember, trials can be held virtually anywhere, from high mountains to inner cities.

Our trials expert, John Olsen, a resident of the Seattle area, has joined with other trials enthusiasts in working with the Seattle parks department to find several urban trials sites. Trials can be run on an endless variety of terrain and require no street closings or police help. They need little room, raise no dust, make no noise, and are generally palatable to city officials once they understand what the heck you are talking about.

So go to it! Trialing is easy to get into, challenging to master, and can be set up anywhere.

Welcome to the Wide World of All-Terrain Touring!

Though the all-terrain bike originated primarily to fit the needs of a small group of Marin County cyclists whose idea of a fun weekend was to engage in bombs-away time trials down a steep and rocky fire road, it has since been adapted to a wide variety of uses. Where once it appeared to be a bike of a highly specialized nature, it has now become standard equipment for the well-rounded rider. For such a person, the ATB serves not as a replacement of the traditional 10-speed road bike but as an addition to it. An all-terrain bike extends your range of cycling territory and provides a high-quality alternative bicycle for utility use.

As the all-terrain bike has grown in popularity and availability, many cyclists have discovered its suitability for touring. Two members of the Rodale Press design and product-testing departments selected all-terrain bikes for a summer, 1984, tour around Moosehead Lake in Maine. They found the bikes excellent choices for traveling the mostly dirt logging-company roads that took them around this large lake. Although they found the bikes ideal for wilderness touring, they found that always being self-reliant did pose some problems and inconveniences. The solution: join a group or supported tour.

The Supported Group Tour

While many tourists enjoy the freedom and challenge of being as self-sufficient as possible, others recognize the advantages of traveling in a group that is accompanied by a motorized, support vehicle. This is especially true where the terrain is rugged though accessible to motorized vehicles. The "super tours" popular in the Sierra and Rocky Mountain areas allow road cyclists to ride all the miles and challenge all the passes they can handle, while a support vehicle takes care of the baggage and the cooking staff.

The roots of the supported off-road tour lie not in the super tour, however, but in the famous Crested Butte to Aspen Tour begun almost a decade ago. This annual, two-day ride had its origins more in a party than a tour and has always had vehicular support, if only because the first bikes used were so prone to disintegration along the rugged route.

The first Crested Butte to Aspen Tour was an impromptu affair. It all began when some residents of affluent Aspen strode up to the bar in the Grubstake Saloon of Crested Butte, a not-so-affluent former mining town, and boasted that they had just ridden over on their motorcycles—not the long way around on paved roads, but the direct, tortuous 40-mile route across 12,700-foot-high Pearl Pass.

Determined not to be outdone, a handful of locals decided to ride their 1- and 3-speed bicycles over to Aspen following the same route. Thanks to a lot of tactical support from friends piloting trucks and jeeps loaded with beer, food, camping equipment, and (sometimes) their bikes, these hardy defenders of the pride of Crested Butte eventually made it to Aspen. Tired but vindicated, they wasted no time announcing their feat publically in one of Aspen's popular drinking places.

This episode might have quietly passed into local history had it not been mentioned in print by a freelance journalist. Many months afterward, a group of Northern California off-road bike enthusiasts, thinking the "tour" to be an annual event, called the Grubstake Saloon and asked permission to join the 1978 ride. The startled saloon keepers said, "sure," and set about recruiting some local riders willing to go along.

Thus it came about that in September, 1978, five Californians and ten Coloradans set out from Crested Butte along the high road to Aspen. Unlike the locals, the Californians were prepared technologically, riding prototype "mountain bikes" and carrying the tools and the skills necessary to make repairs as the tour progressed. The point was not lost on the Coloradans. Since that time, word of this rugged but scenic tour has continued to spread, and it has become a popular and well-established annual event. The town of Crested Butte has, for its part, become a center of off-road bike enthusiasm and activity.

Whereas the original Crested Butte to Aspen tour had as many motor vehicles as bikes, the format for the now institutionalized tour includes the setting up of a campground a day in advance. An experienced cooking staff works for several days in order to feed two meals to the nearly 300 riders currently attracted to the event.

Touring purists may scoff at the idea of having a motor vehicle carry cyclists' gear and food, but there are good reasons for it off road. The "high point" of the Crested Butte to Aspen journey is climbing to the summit of Pearl Pass, nearly 13,000 feet above sea level, over rocks and boulders. Although a few hard-core riders have done this with full sets of panniers, most find it a major struggle just to get an unloaded bike up there.

And the downhill trip isn't much easier; it's hard enough for most people to negotiate it on their bikes, even without gear. Loaded bikes would probably wind up being walked down most of the rugged descent, with their owners struggling to hang on to them.

For the inexperienced off-road rider, a supported tour is an opportunity to check out scenery or try a new bike without the danger of having to walk 20 miles in the case of equipment failure. Even experienced cyclists shouldn't head into the back country alone, and those with less experience are even more subject to the hazards of bicycle damage, injury, or getting lost. The support vehicle can carry full sets of spare parts, tools, and first aid equipment that would be a burden for the riders, especially if they have to cross difficult terrain.

Photograph 4–5. All-terrain bicycle tours let you enjoy sites that traditional cyclists never get to enjoy, unless they are walking.

The presence of a guide is welcome to experienced and inexperienced riders alike. There is an old saying, "the map is flat." Roads or hills that may look passable from the comfort of a living room may in fact be washed out, snowed under, or closed to cyclists. Also, new roads may have been constructed since your map was published, and an experienced guide will know them.

Supported tours come in all sizes, colors, and price ranges, depending on where they go and the philosophies of the leaders. Minimum support may consist of a guide only with riders packing their own gear, but most package tours offer more than this. Some tours would have to be called luxury affairs, with amenities such as hot tubs or bed-and-breakfast accommodations. Others consist of a guide, one support vehicle, and cook; this is a more common arrangement.

An ATB Tour Sampler

Casey Patterson's Southern California operation, Wilderness Bicycle Tours, was the first company offering a regular off-road touring schedule with catered meals. In her three years of tour leading, owner Patterson has noted and responded to a change in the clientele. "At first it was just beginners," she says, "and we had to supply them with bikes and be careful not to take on anything too tough. Now more and more of our customers bring their own bikes and are good enough riders to take on our more challenging tours, where we tackle a 1,500-foot or higher climb every day." Casey also notes that many of her customers are competent road cyclists who may have little experience off the road, but who are in good physical condition and enjoy harder rides.

Wilderness Tours come in a variety of challenges. At the easy end of the scale are 18-mile, mostly downhill, one-day "bird-watching" tours. In the eastern Sierras, Patterson puts on longer trips, up to seven days of moderate to hard riding. One of the 1984 seasons's surprise successes was an all-women's Mother's Day ride in the Point Reyes National Seashore, which according to Casey, will be co-ed in '85. Trips are usually supported by the four-wheel-drive van affectionately called "Mommycar."

Just outside of Helen, Georgia, Koenig's Mountain Madness offers fat-tire access to the Chattahoochee National Forest with an interesting assortment of services. At the low end of the scale, they provide a rental bike and a map, with the option of a day tour with a local rider who acts as a guide. Bike rentals apply to the purchase price of a bike if the rider is so hooked he or she can't leave without one. Another service is the "Shuttle Downhill," a truck ride up and a 2½-hour, ten-mile downhill ride. At the upper end of the scale are two-day rides with cabin lodging, hot tubs, meals, and bikes provided.

In the mountains of Northern Pennsylvania, Mountain Rambles offers rides that range from two-, three-, and four-day camping trips up to a four-day "Inn-to-Inn" tour of country lodgings. Guided routes are from 15 to 20 miles a day, and the route is modified to fit the riders, the weather, or time factor. Side trips or alternate loops through more challenging routes are available if the riders want to test their abilities. In hot weather, trips may also include downriver "tubing" on the longer tours. Services include the use of a bike and helmet (which they expect you to wear), sag wagon, meals, guides, lodging, and transportation of gear. Tours are limited to ten riders, with some age restrictions.

In Arizona, Bicycle Detours operates an ambitious schedule of tours that covers most of the year. Tours are long, most being between 6 and 14 days, and are rated according to the degree of cycling ability necessary: Novice, Beginner, Energetic Beginner, Intermediate, and Advanced. Distances are planned at about 20 miles a day, which the brochures warn can be a lot longer on a mountain road than it is on pavement, but there is also an option of side trips or riding up to 50 miles a day on some routes. Bicycle Detours uses a shuttle to take tourists over areas with less enjoyable riding or few scenic possibilities. Other services offered are bike rental, helmet, sag wagon, cooking, tents, and transportation of gear, as well as guides. Sleeping accommodations range from "no frills" alternatives on some rides to a mixture of camping and more comfortable lodging on others. One tour that is routed by an interesting archeological site includes on the guide staff an expert who assisted in the excavation of the site.

Because all-terrain bicycles are so well-suited for touring in countries lacking extensive paved highways, tour leaders are adopting them for use in many parts of the world. Some areas with guided tours (offering varying levels of support services) of which we are aware are Baja California, the Himalayas, the Andes, China, Australia, and New Zealand. No doubt such tours will soon be available in many other parts of the world.

We have compiled a list of companies that offered ATB tours in 1984 and 1985. Other touring organizations will most likely add ATB tours as interest in them grows, so you may wish to contact touring companies that are not on this list as well.

Some Companies Offering Organized ATB Tours

Arrow to the Sun Bicycle Touring Company
P.O. Box 115
Taylorsville, CA 95983
Ph. (916) 284-6263
ATB tours in northeastern California and Nevada

Bicycle Detours
P.O. Box 44078
Tucson, AZ 85733
Ph. (602) 326-1624
Tours throughout southwestern U.S., Peru, Caribbean

Bicycle Village
39/41 Ghuznee St.
Wellington, New Zealand
Ph. 847512
One- and two-day ATB tours in New Zealand

Bikecentennial
P.O. Box 8308-TN
Missoula, MT 59801
Ph. (406) 721-1776
ATB tours in the western U.S.

Bike Virginia
P.O. Box 203
Williamsburg, VA 23187
Ph. (804) 253-2985
Off-road bike weekend tours in the Shenandoah Valley, Virginia

Blue Ridge Biking
P.O. Box 504
Montezuma, NC 28653
Ph. (704) 733-5566
Off-road camping trips in the Blue Ridge mountains

China Passage Travel Service
302 Fifth Ave., 10th Flr.
New York, NY 10001
Ph. (212) 564-4099
ATB tours of Mongolia

Colorado Bicycle Tours
P.O. Box 45-R
Pitkin, CO 81241
Ph. (303) 641-4240
ATB tours throughout Colorado

Downhill Spokers Bicycle Tours
39 E. 30th St.
New York, NY 10016
Ph. (212) 684-7847
Weekend ATB tours in upstate New York

Epic Educational Expeditions
P.O. Box 209
Sun Valley, ID 83353
Ph. (208) 788-4995
Mountain bike tours in Idaho

Koenig's Mountain Madness
P.O. Box 308
Helen, GA 30545
Ph. (404) 878-2851
ATB tour in the Chattahoochee National Forest

Liberty Bell Alpine Tours
Star Route
Mazama, WA 98833
Ph. (509) 996-2250
ATB tours of the North Cascades

Mountain Rambles
R.D. #1, P.O. Box 308
Hughesville, PA 17737
Ph. (717) 584-2806
Northern Pennsylvania mountain tours

Mystic Wheels
2820 W. Elizabeth
Fort Collins, CO 80521
Ph. (303) 482-3448
Colorado tours

Nantahala Outdoor Center
US19W, P.O. Box 41
Bryson City, NC 28713
Ph. (704) 488-2175
All-terrain tours in North Carolina and Yellowstone Park

Nepalese Mountain Bike Tours
P.O. Box 76007
Washington, DC 20013
Ph. (202) 543-2004
Tours in the mountains of Nepal

San Diego Mountain Bicycle Tours
1831 Missouri St.
San Diego, CA 92109
Ph. (619) 270-0914

Touring Exchange
P.O. Box 265
Port Townsend, WA 98368
Ph. (206) 385-0667
Mountain bike tours in California, New Mexico, and the North Cascades in Washington

Tropical Bicycle Odysseys
26 Abbott St.
Cairns 4870, Australia

Wilderness Bicycle Tours
P.O. Box 692
Topanga, CA 90290
Ph. (213) 455-2544
California ATB tours

Credits

The information in this book is drawn from these and other articles from *Bicycling* magazine plus one other source noted.

"The Race That Gave Birth to the Clunker" Charles R. Kelly, "Clunkers Among the Hills," *Bicycling*, January/February 1979, pp. 40–42; Frank Berto, "Repack Revisited," *Bicycling*, March 1984, pp. 20–21.

"The Vanguard: ATBs and Their California Builders" Charles R. Kelly, "The Vanguard: ATBs and Their Dedicated, Imaginative Band of California Builders," *Bicycling*, March 1985, pp. 126–39.

"All-Terrain Bikes: A Buyer's Guide" Jim Redcay, "Shopping the Buyers' Guide," *Bicycling*, January/February 1985, p. 92; Fred Zahradnik, "ATBs: On Track for Off-Road," *Bicycling*, January/February 1985, pp. 70–74.

"Selecting the Right Gearing for Your ATB" Frank Berto, "All About Off-Road Bike Gearing: Here's How Your Ballooner Needs to Be Geared for Mud, Water, and Steep Hills," *Bicycling*, August 1983, pp. 54–57.

"The City Bike Alternative" The *Bicycling* Staff, "City Bikes: Now Appearing in a Town near You," *Bicycling*, September/October 1984, pp. 80–113.

"Climbing Techniques for Trail Riders" John Olsen, "Hill Climbing for Trail Riders: Out-of-the-Saddle Techniques," *Bicycling*, May 1984, pp. 24–27.

"The Safe Way to Descend Steep Places" John Olsen, "Safe Technique for Steep Descents: Swing Low, Sweet Fat-Tire Bike," *Bicycling*, September/October 1984, pp. 116–19.

"Riding over Logs and Other Large Objects" John Olsen, "Log Jumping for Trail Riders: It's Easy and Fun to Ride over Large Obstacles," *Bicycling*, June 1984, pp. 30–34.

"Riding in Snow" John Day, "Going in Snow: An All-Terrain Bike Can Conquer the Fourth Season," *Bicycling*, November/December 1983, pp. 22–26.

"Off-Road Racing Is Fun for Everyone" Art Read, "Off-Road Racing: More Fun per Mile," *Bicycling*, April 1984, pp. 31–33.

"Observed Trials for Bicyclists" John Olsen, "All-Terrain Trialing: The Idea Is Not to Put Your Foot Down," *Bicycling*, September/October 1983, pp. 33–38.

"Welcome to the Wide World of All-Terrain Touring!" Charles R. Kelly, "Trends: All-Terrain Touring," unpublished manuscript.

Photographs

Carl Doney: photo 3–8; David Epperson: photos 4–4 and 4–5; T. L. Gettings: photo 1–1; Tim Heydon: photos 3–1 and 3–2; Mark Lenny: photo 2–2; Mitchell T. Mandel: photos 1–4, 1–7, and 1–8; Lew Plummer: photos 3–3, 3–4, 3–5, 3–6, 3–7, and 4–3; Photo Dept., Rodale Press: photos 1–2, 1–3, 1–6, and 4–1; Frank J. Staub: photo 4–2; Christie C. Tito: photo 2–3; Sally Shenk Ullman: photos 1–5 and 2–1.